THE *Magic* IN THE *Nightmare* THAT WAS *Me*

a memoir by
DAKODA FOXX

BLUE FORGE PRESS
Port Orchard, Washington

The Magic in the Nightmare that was Me
Copyright 2018
by Dakoda Foxx

First eBook Edition, August 2021
First Print Edition, August 2021
Second Print Edition February 2023

ISBN 978-1-59092-937-7

All rights reserved, including the right to reproduce this book or portions thereof in any form whatsoever, except in the case of short excerpts for use in reviews of the book.

For information about film, reprint or other subsidiary rights, contact blueforgegroup@gmail.com

This is a work of fiction. Names, characters, locations, and all other story elements are the product of the authors' imaginations and are used fictitiously. Any resemblance to actual persons, living or dead, or other real life situations is purely coincidental.

Blue Forge Press is the print division of the volunteer-run, federal 501(c)3 nonprofit company, Blue Forge Group, founded in 1989 and dedicated to bringing light to the shadows and voice to the silence. We strive to empower storytellers across all walks of life with our four divisions: Blue Forge Press, Blue Forge Films, Blue Forge Gaming, and Blue Forge Records. Find out more at www.BlueForgeGroup.org

Blue Forge Press
7419 Ebbert Drive Southeast
Port Orchard, Washington 98367
blueforgepress@gmail.com
360-550-2071 ph.txt

*for my mother, Lillie Thomas,
and my third grade teacher and friend, Wanda Hill*

This book is dedicated to two women who supported me without ever questioning where I was going or who I was going be. Even though the road was hard and crazy at time you never left my side or gave up on me.

I want to thank you for that.

Author's Note

The events and experiences that follow happened. In some places I have changed the names, identities, and other specifics of individuals in order to protect their privacy and integrity and their right to tell their own stories.

The story comes from my recollections and may not be a word-for-word transcript. I did keep the real and true essences, mood, and spirit of the exchanges.

Publisher's Note

To preserve the authenticity and voice of the author, this memoir has been edited lightly for clarity but otherwise left as it was originally written.

Content Warning: Scenes depicting gun violence, kidnapping, rape, domestic violence, physical and verbal assault.

THE *Magic* IN THE *Nightmare* THAT WAS *Me*

a memoir by
DAKODA FOXX

A poem I wrote when I was thirteen years old:

Open Your Window

Your window needs to be open
to hear what's been going on
in and outside your home.
Your child has been neglected
she has been mentally and physically abusing
now she's rejected and withdrawing
from the world.
She used to be
sweet and innocent
but not anymore.
You somewhere in the house
crotch up in the corner
drinking down a bottle of Scotch.
The more you drink
the less you do for your child.
She needs you
she's scared, crying for love
and lots of understanding.

The Magic in the Nightmare that was Me

Your friends are only
caring for that young body of hers
they turned on to alcohol.
What it would take
to search your heart
to seek help for the both of you.
All this world cares about
is themselves
but you know it caused her
to turn to alcohol and not trust
and withdraw from the outside world.
It has forced her to
go down a road that
she didn't want to go.
She won't ever be
the young sweet girl
never again.
She lost her childhood
way back when.
You must open up your window
and if you could
you would've heard
what's been going on
in your own backyard.
Sure it's alright for her to have friends
but you never had time to meet any of them

and didn't even want
anything to do with her.
You were only interested
in the bottle
so that's where she ran
to see
what was at the bottom of the bottle also.
You only wanted to deal with her
when she was playing sports
or winning competitions in school.
You never took the time
to see her for her.
But what will it take
for you to see
the true side
and open your window
and go find your child
and bring her home.
Did you even notice
that she was alone?
Search your heart
and when you see
your window opening
your world could be a better place.

Isn't it time you became a mother?

Preface

Growing up, I had expectations of being everything I wanted to be, yet everything was so far out of our reach. I had hopes and dreams of one day becoming a lawyer, from a very early age of eight. I had people telling me that I could grow up to be anything I wanted to be but then life happens and it starts taking twists and turns. There's nothing to do but ride this rollercoaster till it comes to a complete stop. To get on to the next journey or wait for the next ride.

The people that you grew up thinking was supposed to be there to protect you, are often the ones that hurt you the most. But when you're young, you don't understand that. You grow up to know and see the difference between how people treat you and how you supposed to be treated. When this happens, sometimes your reality and your fantasies get twisted. And the only person that gets trapped and lost is the younger you that was meant to be everything you supposed to be.

But when you're in the thick of things you really can't see how you going to get out of it until it's all done and over with. Sometimes the hardest journey is to retrain your mind to be better than where you came from, as you get your foot going in a direction that you need to go, to make it better. Holding on to the pain and the hurt will only hold you back from getting the blessings that you need and deserve. Sometimes the best thing you need to do is to walk away from situations, people, places, and things that bring you no good.

Until you can separate, too, you will forever be trapped in your own mind. This is not to say that what people have done to you is okay, but holding on to that pain can only bring you more trauma and pain itself than if you would have let it go. No one is perfect in this life but sometimes you have to realize that your life is what matters the most and no pain, no trauma, and no one else can hold you back but you.

When you're destined for greatness all the

trauma and pain that you went through only is just a setback in the lesson to teach you to go into the next part of your life. So you take that and you use that to build you up and build who you are as a person and as a whole. Because you can't let something captivate you so completely and hold you back to where you are stuck in a stagnant state. Then this is where you will stay for years to come. Then you have held yourself back. Then you can't blame no one for being stuck there.

    I have been through a lot of things, but I refuse to be a prisoner in my own mind. And let my abusers or my attackers keep me from being who God put me here to be. I walk through this life now better than I was before. I am here to help someone who has been through this just as I have. I'm here to let them know that it's okay and you will come out alright in the end. There is a light at the end of the tunnel—you just got to keep looking for that light no matter how dark it may be. I'm telling you, there is light. Keep looking. But there's one thing that you got to do if you want to see that light. You have to let all the hurt and anger go. Because holding on to that only will make you sick, angry, and bitter.

No one deserves to be mistreated or abused. And no one deserves to be trapped in their own mind, either. It's okay to let it go. When I sit back and think about it, when I did hold on to it, I was so sick. And I realize then, by letting it go, my life got better. I had to love me more. Now I see the beauty in everyone no matter what the situation. It was like a light bulb that went off in me and I knew that all the stuff that I had been through, I was here to help someone see that it's okay.

Not saying life wasn't hard at those times and not saying that I didn't see the darkness, because I did. It's that I held on to the light just a little bit more. All the comforting things that I could find in my mind to use to get by I did. I turned to music, I turned to painting, I turned to writing. I found outlets that would give me good motivation to step out of the box, step out of the darkness that was trying to creep up on me. I found love within myself, to find love to share with others. I would never say that I would redo my life over because it wouldn't have made me who I am today and I wouldn't have the beautiful kids that I have now. I just know that if I can help anybody through their journey, I will be right there. See, I know how it feels to be abandoned, alone, and going through things that no one can possibly understand. And people tell you how they think you should feel about the situation when they don't even have a clue about how it even feels to be in this situation. And then they want to give you advice about how you should feel.

When you're in a situation that requires a lot of meditation to get through it, just remember there's a light at the end of the tunnel. You may not see it but it's there—you just got to hold on for a few more moments in time. Don't leave your mind for momentarily satisfaction or gratification because sometimes those things hold you back and come find you to where you don't want to be.

And just remember when you are thinking about suicide or anything like that, ask yourself these questions. The first one is: Who will it affect? The second one is: How will it affect them? And the third one in the most important one: If I did this and they were affected, how would their life be without me, the person that meant the most to them?

Sometimes we often think that doing something like this will only affect us and it'll fix the solution right then, but we never look at the ripple effect that we are leaving after we've done it. I just wanted to leave that on your plate for a moment. If you had that point, I would beg you to go and get some help and will find someone to listen. Because sometimes really all we want is to be heard and understood.

I can't express myself more than this: When you feel like you're in the deepest part and there's nowhere to go there's always someone out there just like you that is looking for the same answers. Someone who's going through something similar just like you that you may be the one that could help them through it. Taking that moment to help somebody else—it's hard especially when you're dealing with your own issues. I know I had that happen to me one time but I'm glad I took the time to help. It did not just help them, it actually help me too.

So, while reading this book I hope that you can find it helpful and help you understand that you're not alone. You don't have to be afraid. You don't have to run and hide. You can just be you. Because everybody out there has a story—you just don't know what their story may be. And taking a moment to share your story with someone who is in needed of it is a wonderful thing. It's okay to be you because you're wonderfully made. And we were put here to help each other. There's no such thing as broken pieces. To me, the pieces of the puzzle of life, once you put them all on the table, you'll find that each person fits together like a puzzle. And when you finish, the world would be a big picture made of a puzzle.

So, I wish you luck. Know that you're not alone and know that I love you. I hope this book can help someone and let them know they are not alone. Because I know there are other women out there just like me.

If I can be a blessing to someone that has or is still going through what I went through, and I can offer advice or just a listening ear, I will do whatever I can to help. If there is one thing I can say that I took away from all the things I went though, it was that no matter how hard the road was, the journey of the message I learned was awesome.

I thank everyone that has been there for me though the ups and downs. The ones who was with me on my journey to another life. The pitfalls and the landmines. Because without the learned behaviors and the learned retraining of my mind, I wouldn't be here.

No rewards go unnoticed and no regrets go unturned.

CHAPTER 1
The Fence

Turning thirteen was supposed to be the happiest childhood moment of your life. Well mine was with a twist. I was in the process of getting married to a twenty-eight-year-old man I barely knew. I was already offered before I was born to the family of this man—beyond that, I was pregnant and I had to get married now to make it look like this is what it was.

By the time we finished getting married my family told us that we had a house in the country, land that they had bought for us. This was good in a way—we had a place to stay and we don't have to stay with either of the parents.

So I decided that I would decorate the house and get furniture and stuff for the house and do what I needed to do to be the woman of the house. It was kind of hard because I only had two role models—my grandmother and my mom—but watching them made it seem easy.

I set up the electricity all by myself. He told me that I had to learn how to be the woman of the house, so that's what I needed to do. I took care of all the bills—he brought the check home, kept twenty dollars for himself, and I did everything else. By the time my child came I was already ready.

There was an issue with our arrangement because no one knew that I was a lesbian and he was gay. Our family said that we had to have one biological child. So, we decided to work on that after my child came.

My newly-found husband decided to raise my child as his own. I had been raped, and he knew about it. A couple of his friends was at the house when it took place, they tried to help but they didn't get there in time. See, my rapist had gone around town bragging about all of how he did it and how now he's about to be a father. And everybody knew that this had happened, but my husband was very understanding, and he stepped up to the plate and became my child's father.

As time went by, I knew the cards that I was dealt, and I knew my place. I was thirteen and running the house, working and holding down the house with kids. This was a lot, but I did it. My husband was a good man. But he didn't understand that I still was a child. Even thought I was his wife, I was still a thirteen-year-old girl.

We would argue and fight because he thought I was being childish and didn't understand things. I told him often that I'm learning and don't know a lot of things to do as an adult. So we would bump heads.

One day we got into a fight. He was like *You don't know what you're doing.*

I told him *You're so right. I don't know but you should show me instead of yelling.*

But he wanted to just yell, so I walked away and he yanked me and pulled me back saying *You are not going anywhere.* He slapped me so hard and said *You got to stay in your place.* This was the first time he had done this, and I didn't understand what was going on. In my mind it was like kids on the playground hitting you and you got to stand your ground, or they will keep on.

So I yanked back and said *Don't put your hands on me.*

He was like *No, you are going to listen to me.*

I walked away and then went into the bedroom and called my friend. I had asked her if she could come and get me. I asked if she could take me to my mom's house. I called my mom and told here I was on my way.

She asked *What happened?*

I told her *I will tell you when I get there.*

I had to gather the kids stuff and get them ready so we could go. I couldn't find the blankets but that was okay. I waited for thirty minutes because we lived so far from town and in the *county* county.

My friend was outside. I went out the back door thinking since he was in the front watching football, he wouldn't hear me.

But as soon as I got the kids in the car and was about to get in, he comes out yelling at me. *Where do you think your going and with my kids? Get your ass back in this house.* He was saying *You're not going to take my kids anywhere. Take the kids out the car. Woman you are not going anywhere.*

This was the first time he had referenced me as a woman and not a child. He always treated me like a woman and wanted me to act like a woman all the time but had always called me a child.

She started to drive off and he yelled even more. As we was driving down the path he was running saying *Come back.* He was sorry.

As we was driving to my mom's house, my friend turned to me and said *You really don't need this and you need some ice on your eye and your face.*

I didn't realize that I had a black eye and a hand print on my face. She said *Why do you let him do this to you?* I said this was the first time. She said *You know if he does it once he will do it again.* I told her I knew that.

As we got closer to my mom's house I had to think of what I was going to tell my mom. I pulled up and got the kids out the car and took them inside. By the time we got inside, my friend's mom called and said *Your husband called and ask was we there.* She said *What's going on? Why is he looking for you and why don't he know were you are?* I told her the things that had happened, and she said *Honey, you have to get out—this* is just the beginning. Get out now, I don't want to see you hurt.

I got in the house and sat the baby in the play pen and took my other little one to the play room. Came back and my mom let me have it. She asked what happened. I told her that he yanked me and hit me. She said *Honey he does it once he will do it again.*

I told her *Yes, I know, mom.*

The phone ring started ringing off the hook. She slowly went to answer it, first asking *I know this is your husband. What do you want me to tell him?* I told her to tell him I was here, and I was okay, and I would be home tomorrow sometime. She answered it and sure enough it was him. She said he wanted to know if I was here. My mom told him what I said, and he said that he was going to come get me that night.

She told him why both of you don't cool down tonight and meet up tomorrow. He said *No, I am on my way. Please tell her to be ready.*

Not too long after, he pulled up to my mom's house. He came up to the door knocking and my mom answered the door and said *She told you that she was coming home tomorrow.*

He stood at the door and kept saying that he

wanted me home now. He wasn't leaving until I came out here and talked to him.

My mom said *You should calm down and try to get some sleep tonight and come get her and the kids tomorrow.*

He said *No, we need to talk now. This is all my fault. I know this. I never meant to hurt her. I just want to talk to her.*

I walked up to my mom and put my hand on her shoulder and said *It's okay, Mom. I am going to go outside and talk to him for a moment. I will be back. Can you watch the kids for me?*

She said *Of course I can.*

I went out side and sat in the yard and talk to him. He started to apologize to me and said he don't know what's got into him. I said I didn't understand what was going on. He said he didn't know either. He said he think he was scared because the baby was due soon and he felt he wasn't making enough money to take care of three kids and us too.

We weren't struggling—we was fine. We didn't need anything. The bills were paid. We had all the things we needed. We had food and clothes for all of us. All the kids had milk and Pampers. So, I really didn't understand what he was worried about.

He looked at me with them sad light brown eyes and I knew he was sorry. We were such the best of friends. And he didn't want to leave without telling me he was sorry. He needed to hear my voice. He knew I was okay by the tone of my voice. We sat there for a few more moments and then he asked me *So are you coming home tonight?*

I looked at him and said *No dear, not tonight. I am going to stay here and hang with my mom tonight. Plus she is enjoying the grand kids. So I will be home tomorrow. Come get me when you get off of work. We will be ready.*

We sat out there for about thirty more minutes and talked about what we would do next. He said *Are you cooking tomorrow, or should I pick up something on my way to come pick you and the kids up?* He asks *May I see my kids before I leave?*

I said *Sure, you silly man. You can always see your kids. No matter how mad I get at you they didn't have anything to do with us arguing. Unless you put your hands on them and then I am going to knock your ass out. That is the truth. Those babies are my world.*

He looked and said *I know they are. I would never hurt them. They are my world too.*

Good, because I didn't want to have to take you out, I said.

As we got up to go into the house my mom came out and said *You better come here.*

I go in the room and they was play fighting. My oldest was smacking the middle one. I looked at him and said *See? Even when you think they wasn't paying attention, kids watch everything. So my oldest saw you hit me. So now they think it's okay. That's not cool.*

My husband got mad all over again. And said *I never meant for this to happen.*

I looked at him and said *We never meant for things to happen, but they do. We supposed to be leading by example. Now you know that they are watching your every move.*

So he left and went home and he called me about five times before he went to sleep. It was unusual for him to keep calling and checking up on me. I didn't know what to think about this at all. The whole day was off.

So that day, he went to work and then got off, came straight to me and didn't pick up any food. He came to my mom's house and said that he just wanted to see me. I said *You can see me anytime.*

He said *Let's go in here and get the kids and go to the store to get dinner.* Then he asks me *Are you going to your girlfriend's house later tonight?*

I said *No, why?*

He said he just wanted to spend time with me. I really didn't know what was going on with him, but he wanted to spend time with me and just watch TV. This was something new to me.

We got back home, and I cooked and got the kids ready for bed. He came in and just looked at us. This went on like this for a while. I didn't know whether it was because of what had happened when he hit me but things did change that day after that. He became my husband and I became his wife.

We were even attending parties our friends had put on. We were getting closer and I didn't know what was happening. I did embrace it and loved every moment of it. He was stuck on me like glue. This went on for about five to six months. He even went with me to my doctor's appointments.

It was getting close to my due date and I was getting ready for this baby. I cleaned the whole house. I just may have over done it or something. The day of the birth went well and the baby was healthy and all.

But then, later on that day, I felt really weird and I was calling the nurse in the room, but I guess I didn't do it fast enough. I was having a heart attack. The doctors didn't know what it came from. One doctor said it was stress related.

They let me come home five days later due to the heart attack. After that things turn back to normal. I went back to school and he went back to work. We rarely saw each other besides Fridays when he came home from work to bring his check.

We both had someone else, so it wasn't a thing for us. I loved women and he love his guy he was with. But we loved each other. We became the best of friends. We talked about anything and everything. I got pregnant and had my baby and all was going well. We had just got new neighbors and they was a white couple. It was okay for the first few months.

Then, it became a issue when my husband got a dog and she was about to have puppies. I think the dog had about eight puppies, and my neighbor kept asking my husband, could he have one? And my husband said, no. He was selling them, he wasn't giving them away. He said *You could pay for one if you wanted one.*

But the guy said, no. He don't want to pay for any puppies. He said *It would be very neighborly-like if you gave us one for a house warming gift,* and of course my husband said no.

Things got very interesting after that. His wife kept coming over to our side checking the dog and doing something over on our property so we decided that we was going to put up a temporary fence. That did not go well—he kept coming back and forth over to the property and finally decided that he wanted to get on his big riding lawn mower and knocked the fence down.

So, my husband's boyfriend came to the house. He stood six foot eight and was built big. He was trying to reach over and put the fence back together— he was tall enough to not only reach the top of the wire that went up to the to the pole but also tall enough to reach over and bend over and pull to the post without getting stuck. He also tried to stretch out the part that the next-door neighbor broke with his riding lawn mower.

We decided that we would try to get some help with the situation. When we did call the cops they was telling us that we couldn't put up a fence around our property because it was disturbing the neighbors. I said *What if the neighbors put up a fence? Could we call the cops because it was disturbing us?*

He said *No,* so I said *So there's a double standard here.*

He said *Just don't put up a fence.*

A month went by. The puppies was getting bigger and they were almost ready to go to the proper homes. We decided that we was going to keep the puppies inside due to the fact that our neighbors was really doing the most around our property. You figured four acres was big enough for it to keep them off our land. It wasn't like you could just walk out your door directly into somebody else's house like apartment. We didn't know how to keep him off the property and the law was not on our side because we was the wrong color.

On a late February evening I was cooking and cleaning and washing clothes at the same time and also trying to get the kids ready for bed. I don't think I'll ever forget this.

I was in the kitchen, cooking and trying to make sure that everybody was getting enough to eat. In the front room my husband was sitting there watching TV with our kids. My oldest was walking around, playing in the living room and the other bedroom. My husband was holding my youngest because I told him that I don't want her to just sit in the car seat the whole time or in the playpen—he needed to start holding her. That's what he did, he had her on his lap, bouncing her up and down as I was cooking around the corner in the kitchen.

The front door was in between the living room and the kitchen, but there was a divider between the kitchen and the living room, so you couldn't see directly into the front room from the kitchen. You had to walk out of the kitchen to get to the living room. As I'm cooking, I heard the front door open and didn't think anything of it. I thought that my husband had just got up to shut the screen door that normally pops open every now and then.

I heard a loud pop followed behind three more pops. I didn't realize that these was gunshots. I never dealt with guns before, so I didn't know what they had sounded like up close and personal.

I ran around the corner and I saw my neighbor standing over my husband and he shot one more time. My baby was still holding on to her dad as he lay there dying. I grabbed my baby and then grabbed my other baby and ran up the street to get help.

As I was leaving the neighbor ran out the house to he and his wife's house and got his shotgun. He started shooting at me and my kids. I tried not to look back, I just tried to keep going just in case a bullet had hit us. I had embraced them in front of me and shielded them so if a bullet did hit me it wouldn't hit them at all. This man was crazy.

I'm banging on the door of my neighbor, saying *Please help, my husband's been shot! Please calls the police!*

My neighbor came out and he said *What?*

I said *My next-door neighbor shot my husband, can you please call the police? He's trying to shoot us, he's running towards us with the shotgun!*

He said *Come in, come in, come in, please.*

As he is shutting the door my neighbor came up banging on his door and said *Let the black bitch out! You don't need to hold and harbor them. We will get the bitch, trust that. Once you come out we going to shoot her dead. You can keep the kids, we just want her.*

They called the police for us. The police went to my house. My husband was dead, had been shot eight times at point blank range. My neighbor who shot him was taken into custody and they didn't even waste any time tell me that the fence is what made the neighbor have an issue with me. They tried to fine us for selling a dog but realized that we still had all eight dogs. The judge apologized and said that he was sorry he got misinformation from the police officers.

The judge gave my neighbor five years for the murder of my husband. He got out in two. I had lost faith in the system. I felt like that no matter what we did it would have come out the same way. Who was going to protect us from the police and the justice system when it came to my race? There was no justice and that made me want to be a lawyer that much more.

Later that year I couldn't take it anymore. I shut down and became a fan of Johnnie Walker. He was my best friend at the time. I didn't care anymore. I had just turned seventeen and being mad at the world was my main goal. I lost my best friend in the world, even thought we were forced to become one. Being young and not understanding this and confused how to process this was hard. I had to go. I left my kids with my mom and told her I was going to the store and left. I got on a Greyhound bus and didn't look back. I had clothes for a week and a bottle of Johnnie Walker. I did this for the next two years. I didn't call my mom or let her know I was alive or anything.

I knew this was bad, but I just needed to get away and be free and get away from myself. I was mad at myself because I felt I should have done something more to save him.

So running was my way to escape. I kept finding more places to go by the end of the two years. I had lived in every state but Maine. I kept moving to run away from me... but there was nowhere to go that I wouldn't be there.

I was tired of running, living life on the edge and just moving from place to place, never having anything to call my own.

I settled down in a city that I fell in love with. Just in the nick of time I decided that I would focus on going to college. I went to a college for auto mechanics at first, then I decided that wasn't for me. Then I changed to home builder and finished that, then went for chemical engineer, then criminal justice, then computer science, then legal and politics.

I came home to see my kids and my mom. It

felt good to be home. After two years in hotels and other people homes, my bed felt amazing. I had missed my kids. My baby was five months old when I left and now she was all big and walking and talking. I stayed with my mom for a few weeks and then I had to go find work.

I left and headed for the city to see if I could look for a place and work. I found a job and it was close to the place I wanted to stay at.

CHAPTER 2
The Luck

It's five o'clock and I'm sitting in the blazing hot sun in the back yard of my apartment. I just got home to relax from work. I wave to my next-door neighbor and she walks into her home from work also. I'm sitting there thinking that this is going to be a long night. As I heard the gunshots ranging from the front of the house, a dog hides down behind the garbage can, and my neighbor comes back out and asks *Are you okay?*

I say *Yes, I'm doing just fine.*

She says *They been doing this a lot lately.*

I say *Yes, as long as they keep it on the other side,*

they'll be good.

As she was just about to go inside her home, we heard two more shots. She turned to me and looked and said *I think I got stung by a bee.* I got up and walked over to her as she fell to the ground, gasping for air. I went running inside to grab my cell phone to call 911.

As I came back out with my cell phone, calling 911 in the process, I did not realize that she had got shot between her ribs which had collapsed her lungs. I was pressing on the wound to stop the bleeding but that was not working because it was kept coming through. Finally, the ambulance came and then they took her to the hospital.

I finally went back inside to see what was going on in the front of the house. There was two other people who had got hit, also. This was crazy to me. She was just out here talking to me.

I waited for her kids to get home from school from the after-school program. I had dinner cooked and everything ready for them. My neighbors' daughters came home and I told her to come over and eat, and that her mom would be back later, and that they would have to stay with me until her mom got back. This wasn't unusual because she normally stayed over and had a sleepover when her mom got too drunk to be at home or to let her in the house. She had clothes here already to go to school the next day.

She went upstairs to play after eating dinner. And I was on the phone with the hospital to see how Gaga was. They said that she was in critical condition. The bullet had pierced her lungs and collapse them, so she was in ICU. I tried to get ahold of her daughter to see if she could get her sisters and she did come to get them.

As the kids was going to school the next morning I decided not to go to work and I went to buy me a big bottle of Johnnie Walker. I took the bus, crossed the bridge to the nearest water and sat there all day until it was dark and I was on my third bottle.

This was my routine for a while. I went to work, bought a bottle, cooked and then went to work. This was my repeat for a while. I was stuck in a bottle for the majority of that year which made me make very poor decisions and judgments.

CHAPTER 3
The Hurt

On my way home from work one day, I hear someone yell out. I turn around and I look and there was a woman over by the corner store. She was just standing there yelling at a man in a blue Mustang. He was throwing her stuff out of the window and calling her all kinds of names and she was yelling back telling him *You're no good.* I turned around and walk back towards the corner store that I had already passed, seeing that she was crying.

I went back and asked if she was okay? She's like, *Yes, I'm fine thank you.*

She was gathering her stuff that he had thrown

out on the ground. I bent down to help her pick up and gather her stuff. She looked up at me with those big brown eyes through her glasses, slightly tilted on her nose, coming halfway down her face. And I asked *Well how far you are going? You can't possibly carry all this stuff by yourself.* I offered to help take some stuff to her house.

As we walked the longest five blocks of my life, I said *Was that your boyfriend?*

She says *Yes, my ex to be exact. He left me for his baby mama.*

I said *That's unfortunate. Some men are stupid and that's why they lose out on good things—because they're stupid.*

She said *Yes, that is true, but he won't miss me because he has his baby mama and that's what he wanted.*

I said *Yes, but even though that's what he thought wanted, if it was truly what he really wanted, he would not leave her in the first place.*

She looked up at me and said *You're probably right. He's just going wherever he can, to get what he needs for the night. He's not coming back here.*

We sat and talked for hours. Found out her name was Megan and she was from the north side of

New York. I said *How about that, I have no clue where the north side is, but I have family there.*

She was in the sergeant in the Military. She said that she worked on the other side on the Bayside. I told her I had just joined not too long ago. She said *Cool.* We had that in common. She thanked me for helping out and asked me, was I hungry, and she decided that she wanted to cook for me.

She started cooking. It was rice, steak, and green beans. How simple was that dinner—it was good. She was like *So do you live around here?*

I say *Yeah. I live five blocks from you around the corner.*

She's like *Oh cool, that's not far at all.*

I said *No, it's not.* Just like this whole time we've been talking I realize that we were closer than we know.

So what is your name?

I said *My name is Joe.*

Nice to meet you, Joe. She checked what I was going to do for the rest of the night. I said probably go home watch TV and have me a drink. As I got up to walk towards the door, she asks *What are you doing tomorrow?*

I said Nothing much. Same thing I did today: nothing, go home after work, watch TV, have me a drink.

She said No, tomorrow you will be over here for dinner and we can watch TV together. So, I guess we'll have to thank you for helping me today and making me feel better.

I said, 'I thought you already did that—you cooked dinner.

She said Nope. That was just dinner for today. I have to do another thank you dinner And thank you properly tomorrow when I have more time. I will pick up groceries tomorrow on my way home from work. See you, then, say around six?

I said Okay, see you then.

I got off from work with great anticipation, waiting for six o'clock to come around. I got so excited and nervous at the same time. As I got on the bus, I was thinking this could be a good thing or bad thing.

I was leaving off base and I saw her—she was waiting on the bus as well. We both looked up at each other and I waved and said hello. As I got closer to the stop, I was thinking, should I keep going or should I just stop? I get off, heading down the street towards her house. She said *Let's go to the store and get the food that we need. Then we can head back, and I can start cooking for you.*

This made me even more nervous than I already was. I said *Okay*, with a light grin.

She said *So, how was your day?*

I said *It was great. I'm a little tired but I'm okay, thanks for asking.* I asked *So how was your day?*

She said *It was fine. Are you ready to eat?*

I said *Yes, I am starving.*

As we was eating she said *Would you like to watch a movie?*

I was going to say no... but I said yes. We wanted to watching Boys in the Hood which was one of the strangest thing in the world because picking that movie it made me think of me as a fourteen year old girl and then she asks me *You okay?*

We watched the movie for a while and then I decided to go home. She asked me, would I like to come back for dinner tomorrow I told her maybe another day, not tomorrow and then she's like *Okay, cool.*

As I was walking home which was a couple of blocks from her, I heard shots ring out. They remind me of Gaga when she got shot. There was two men shooting down the way from where I was going.

As I was getting closer to the house, I stop by Gaga's house to see what was going on at the moment. There was nothing going on—she wasn't home, but her daughter was there with her sister trying to take care of her sister and her daughter. She said *My mom is still in ICU. Hopefully she'll pull through.*

I said *I will be praying for her.*

I went in the house and got comfortable for the night, then woke up to a loud banging on the door. I got up, frantically running to the door to see who it was. It was my friend Aiki. He's like *Come quick, it's Brian.*

I ask *What's going on?*

He said *Brian was shot and it's really bad. Him and Davenport was on the corner and both got shot sitting there. Thank you, okay, I got to go.*

I yelled out *This is crazy! What the heck is he doing on the corner, when he said he was supposed to be going home after work? Why was he on the corner with Davenport?*

Aiki said Black shot them.

What the heck is Black doing out there?

He said *I don't know. He got out early.*

I was thinking how long he has been out, 'cause this could be very detrimental to all of us.

Going back three months prior to now, Black was a neighbor of our boyfriend. He used to sit on the porch and sell drugs in front of the house my children still live in. They would come up sometime on the weekend.

So one day, my kids and Gaga's daughter was outside playing and Black was out there selling drugs when someone walked up and shot him. After Black got out of the hospital, I confronted him, and I told him, I said *I do not appreciate you doing that in front of the children. This is not a good look. They shouldn't be seeing this. The kids play out here, this is their area and you know this.* The playground was not too far away from my house—you could see the playground from my door. So with that said, I asked him *Please do not do this in front of the kids or around here, around the playground any longer.*

So he said *Okay* then him and Gaga got into it about him selling drugs around the back of our house. Gaga ratted him out and told the police officer that him and a couple other people were selling drugs from the back of the house around the playground area.

This started a full out war with Gaga and Black. He was locked up and kept sending word to Gaga that she was going to get it. This made me worry that when he got out he would try to retaliate or do something but I knew that he was locked up so we didn't have anything to worry about. They said that he had three years so we was okay with that.

This takes me back to now where Gaga's shot and Black's out. This makes me think that he shot her.

We headed to the hospital to check on Brian, to figure out how all this ties in to what's happening. Brian and Davenport was not at the house that day doing the confrontation. The only people that was at the house was Gaga, Aiki, and Jimmy.

At the hospital, everyone was there waiting for us. Doctor said that they would make it. Brian got shot in the back and Davenport got shot in the leg. This was a blessing that both of them would pull through.

Megan came rushing to the hospital. She had heard someone had got shot and that somebody was banging at my door. She didn't know what was going on so she thought it was me. Now, this is a woman that I've known barely four days. She comes rushing to the hospital to see if I was okay. This was strange but sweet.

Everybody went back and we saw Davenport and Brian. We made sure that they was okay. They would be coming home soon, so we left and went home ourselves to get some sleep and come back tomorrow.

Megan and I left together. I went back to her house to make sure she was okay and got back safe. Then I walked home. She really didn't want me to leave, she wanted me to stay asleep on the couch for the night. But I left anyway and walked home.

The next day we all met up at the hospital. Talked about the weather for about a couple hours and made our way down to the local bar we always met at. It was a local gentlemen's bar that let me in — even though I was the only woman that was allowed to come in. It was kind of nice because none of the men messed with me and they knew I was there.

There was a lady there that I would frequently go see and get lap dances and private dances from. Her name was Erin. I often went there to see her and to make sure that she was okay and got home safe after work. I always order the same thing: a Dr. Pepper on ice with two limes. Always sat at the far corner of the bar facing towards the front door. I had a view of all four mirrors—the two from the front and the two from the back—so I had easy access to see all exits at one time. That's the reason why I sat in that chair. When I came in, everyone knew if they were sitting in that seat they had to get up because that was my seat. My name was actually carved into it by Erin.

Sitting there, we see two people come in, one going to the left of us and one going to the right. Stopping halfway, one of the guys looked at the other and shook his head. I stood up immediately, look at Aiki and said *Let's go.* He said no. I said *Why the hell not? The two goons are in here and we need to leave.*

Aiki said *Well, safer in here then we are out there.* I said okay but if anything happens I'm running. He said *Fair enough. Sit down and enjoy your Dr. Pepper.* Aiki sat there watching the two guys as they try to decide what they're going to do. We was there for almost three hours trying to figure out whether we should leave or stay and finally the guys gave up. They walked around the bar once and then they left.

As I was leaving we saw one of the regulars

that normally come in that knew us. He says *Be careful, they're out there looking for Gaga. They thought that guy was with you so that's why they was combing the streets looking.*

Aiki said *No, she's not with us. She don't hang with us.*

The regular said *I know that but they don't know that.*

As we was walking to the bus stop to catch the bus back to my side of town, we ran into Lucius. He was one of the biggest, baddest drug dealers out there. He ran the streets like it was his children. No one messed with him and if you was okay with him you was good, you was safe.

So Lucius said *You good rooster.* That's what he used to call me. He said he couldn't call me a cock because I didn't have balls, so he called me a rooster because my nuts are the size of a building. He said everyone knows not to mess with you. He said *I've already put that word out there so if you have any trouble, come to me personally, or send word for me and I will come.*

As we was leaving, heading back to my place after leaving Lucius, I turned to Jimmy and said *This is turning out to be one helluva day.*

Jimmy said *You did alright today. You got protection from Lucius. There's no Gaga in our group. You always got the finest chick in the gentlemen's bar and you got this new girl named Megan. So you doing alright for yourself. Helluva day, yeah, but you always come out on top.*

We get to my house and there's a guy on my step. He was like *Do you know where I can find Brian?*

I said, *Who is asking?*

I am Ralph Mader, investigating what happened to him.

Brian doesn't live here so I don't know for sure. He's probably still at the hospital, did you check there?

He answered *No, I did not because people were saying that you are his friend and you would know where he was at.*

I said *Well, I just told you. He's at the hospital.*

We all go inside, we're drinking and we're having a good time. As the night goes on everyone decided that they was going to spend the night.

The next day, we wake up and we go back to the hospital, check on Brian. We do our thing back at the gentlemen's club, have a few drinks, look at a couple of girls, and then off we go. We get back to our neck of the woods and we run into Black.

He asks *Where is Gaga now? I wanted to talk to her last night.*

I said *I don't know where she is. The last time I checked she was at the hospital. I don't know, I haven't talked to her since she got shot.*

He was like *I thought you hung with her.*

I said *She's my neighbor, that's it. The people that you see me with right now besides Brian and Davenport, those are my crew. Those are the people that I hang out with. You don't see me hanging with her, you see me talking to her outside of her house when she comes outside. When she sits on the porch I have no choice but to talk to her. That doesn't mean that were friends or that we're buddy-buddy, that means that we're neighbors. So please don't confuse the two.*

He looked at me strange and then he said *Alright* and he walked away.

That evening I decided to go to Megan's house for dinner. We have been seeing each other regularly these days. Instead of just dinner I began to see her for dinner and spending the night. We wasn't calling ourselves an item yet but we was close to it.

I don't know how many times I have been over

to her house and I did not realize that she had a fifteen year old son. I asked *Where did he come from?*

She's like *Oh, he's always been here* and I said but he never ate dinner with us and she said *Yes, because he's always out with his friends or doing whatever. I always leave him a plate in the microwave and he eats it when he comes home late at night.*

I said okay. So I met him that day for the first time. It was fun and awkward because we liked some of the same things, we did a lot of the same things, and he was cool with me being a woman. I was making this her very first lesbian relationship. She had never wanted to come out because she was afraid of what everybody else was going to say. But she said when she met me, she didn't care what people saw or thought. She told me that she wanted me to meet her brother and her uncle. Those were the only two family members that she had in-state. I said *Oh yeah, that's cool. When I get time, we can all meet up.*

We sat and watched TV for a while and then went to bed. That morning I got up and went to the hospital to see Brian and Davenport. They both was doing okay. I ran into Gaga—she was being released and going home. I told her of all the things that was going on and how Black was looking for her and was out. She told me she wasn't worried about that. She told me that his girl knew where she was and had told her that he isn't mad just wanted to clear the air. I looked with disbelieved and said *Are you sure?*

She was happy and bubbly and said *Yeah, girl, things are okay now. It cool. Don't worry so much, things will be okay.*

As I watched her walk to the elevator door and walk in I didn't realize that it was going to be the last time I'd see her. She went home and sat on her porch like always. Black came by her house and they talked. She must have known that something was going to happen because inside my screen door she left me her keys and her cell phone to call her daughter. From what people said Black and her talked for about thirty minutes on the porch. Then he shot her in the shoulder, and she shot him in the leg. There was several exchanged shots between the both of them. They said it was total of eighteen gunshots in the both of them. Both were found dead on the porch and the argument was all because of the kids' safety in the park.

I went to bar that evening and that's when Erin

told me of what happened. I was in disbelief but then my boys showed up and told me the same thing. I was like *I just saw her. Damn.* Black's boys was in the place too. They had just heard and ran out.

CHAPTER 4
The Deal

Later that day we all went to the south side to visit my sister. She lived off the bus line, so we walked about two miles and half to her place. It was okay because on the way, there was always something to see.

I love spending time with my sister. It is always so much fun. As we got closer to my sister's, Aiki was like *What are we going to do later tonight?*

I was like *I really don't know. Maybe we can go dance till dawn and then go to my place and play cards.* They all said *Okay.* My sister wasn't home yet, and I needed her to come soon. I need to get some clothes and shoes. I needed to look good tonight.

My sister's always late and never on time for

anything. She told me to be here at three. Now it's almost four.

She pulls in the driveway and says *What are you doing?*

I yell *Waiting on you!*

She says *You're early.*

I say *No, you're late, woman.*

She says *Okay, let's go so you can get your stuff. I'm heading back into town if you all want a ride.* I grabbed my stuff and we all got into her car and headed back.

At my house, we was getting dressed for the night, looking good and waiting on everyone else to come back over so we could go out.

Megan come knocking at the door and asked *What're you doing?*

I was like *Me and my boys are going out tonight. I will see you tomorrow, okay? I will hit you up soon or maybe I will come by tonight after we are done.*

I didn't want to tell her where we were going because I didn't want her to show up there. I needed a night out without her. Then, my boys came in and she was leaving. She was upset that I didn't invite her to go but I needed time away from her, for just a moment. I just needed to breathe.

We got to the club and it was popping. We always have a great time there. I always go to my spot in the back by the three-way mirrors. Looking at everyone even when I'm not facing the front. The club was getting packed and my boys was like *It's popping tonight, right?*

I said *The night's still young.*

There were a few people we knew that was regulars and they came and said *Sorry to hear about Gaga, how are you holding up?*

I said *I'm fine thanks.* She said *Let me by you a drink.* I looked at her and said *Sure.* We talked all night even danced with all three of them. This was a fun night. Everyone was having fun and the drinks kelp coming.

I was not drunk but feeling good. The club closed at four and we always close the club out. We shut it down and it was great.

We were outside in front on the sidewalk between the buildings. I was walking across the street when the girl asked me *Come here for a moment.* As we were leaving the club she stood there and asked me *Where we was going now?* She said *I have enjoyed your* company and would like to continue this night back at my place. She asked me *Do you have a girlfriend?* She said *I want to take you home with me and do things you never dream of.* She was cute and was very attractive, but I had to pass on this because I did have a girlfriend.

I told her *You're very pretty and all, but I do have a girlfriend. I can't really, I can't.*

She said *Well, here is my number I you change your mind or ever want to go out, I'm here for you, baby.*

As I was walking away on the sidewalk to go back over there with my friends, I heard a loud screeching sound and brakes squealing. I hear the girl yell *Watch out!* Not thinking I look back at her and didn't realize she was yelling at me. I thought she was yelling at her friends who was in the road.

But she was yelling at me. There was a transfer truck that was coming down the hill that had lost his brakes. He was out of control and headed straight toward me on the sidewalk. He had lost the capability to control the wheel and had no way to stop.

As I got closer to the building where my friends were, they were running. I was like, *What the heck is wrong with you? I didn't get the cooties from that girl—I didn't even kiss her, shit. Why are you running?*

Soon as I got to the corner, I felt a pain in my back. It was the worst pain in the world. Having a baby didn't even come close to this pain. It was out of this world. *Your eyes were bulging out of your head* Aiki would tell me later.

I looked down and noticed I was lifted off the ground but didn't realized that I was being hit by a truck. I then said to my friend *This fucking hurt, man, but look at me, I'm flying.* He is yelling my name loudly. I'm like *What is wrong with him?*

Finally, I came to a loud stop. People was all around me, calling my name and yelling at this dude that was kneeling down, crouching over me, asking me *Are you okay*?

I looked up and said *Yeah, I was flying, did you see me?*

He said *Yes, hold on, I'm going to get you some help*.

As I passed out from the pain my friends were trying to get me some help. I was pinned between the building and the tree. The ambulance comes, and I woke up freaking out. There was three men there: one that looked like Santa Claus, one that looked like Jet Lee, and the last looked like Magic Mike. I was like

What in the world is happening? Did I wake up on a TV show, am I pranked or something? Where did Magic Mike come from? I didn't care, I was like, *Oh my he is pretty.* I was stuck.

I looked up and said, *Jet Lee is cute too.* Then I passed out again. I woke up to Santa Claus pounding on my chest. I woke and said *Did you bring me any toys.*

He looked at me and chuckled. *No dear I didn't, but I did bring you some oxygen.* He put it on my face and then it was like we were flying but they was lifting me up on to the ambulance. I didn't know that I broke my leg and my ribs. I was trying to get up to see us flying.

Everyone was yelling *Stay down*! We were riding to the hospital but I just wanted to go home. I wanted out of this box. Shit, I thought they had tricked me. We were not flying nor was we seeing beautiful women. Santa didn't bring me any toys. So, what was we doing here?

As soon as I get to the hospital my boys were already there. I was like *How you get here so fast, man*? *I know Santa didn't give you a ride because he was playing with his mask on my face the whole time we were riding.*

As they was moving me off the sled the pain became unbearable. I start to cry out. I finally realize that I'm hurt, and the pain is setting in. I pulled off this face mask—Who needs this thing?—I need something or someone else.

I asked the nurse who came in *What happened, what did I hurt?*

She said *You was hit by a transfer truck and you got a broken leg and you a few broke ribs. Now how is your pain on a scale of a 1 to 10?*

I said *100, there is no 10.* I was delirious from the pain and not really realized what is going on. But I'm looking around and look down and said *I can't feel my legs though, can you tell me where they went, are they still there?*

She looked at the other numbers and said *Oh my God, we need to call the doctor ASAP.*

I looked at them and I said *Is this bad?*

She said *The doctor will come in and talk to you.*

Everything from my waist up was hurting and my back was on fire. They said that there was nothing that they could do but give me pain pills until the doctor came in to see what was happening with me. That night was rough. I couldn't take it anymore and asked the nurse *Could you please call the doctor I need something right now?*

Jimmy called my mom and she came up with the kids. I didn't know that he called her but I was glad that he did. I needed her—she made me feel much better. I really didn't want to cry in front of my kids, but I was in so much pain that I couldn't see straight.

My mom made sure that the doctors was treating me right. I was going to surgery tomorrow for my leg and my mom was on it. She made sure that everything was going well. My sister came in to help my mom with the kids. This was good because Mom had help and then she could also tend to me.

My mom stayed with my sister and when she came back the next day for my surgery, my leg was broken in two places and they had to reattach ligaments and joints, they said. My mom was worried because after surgery my leg was still bleeding a lot but they said that this was normal especially with the way the bone had set against my skin.

I was in so much pain I couldn't even think straight to asked what they would do with my ribs. But I guess my mom was already ahead of the game.

She had asked for me and they said that my ribs would have to heal on their own. They gave me a wrap to wrap my stomach and my chest up. With the wrap I was able to breathe better.

I still wasn't able to move my legs nor was I able to stand on my own. I wasn't able to walk and this was very scary for me. I was so afraid.

Megan found out where I was at and she came to the hospital. She came rushing then yelling *Oh my poor baby*. She came and gave me a big ass kiss and was holding me and crying and she kept kissing me all over.

At the same time my first sergeant was walking through the door. He looked at me and asked, *Private, what's going on here?* Well, I couldn't really hide it. The look in her eyes told it all that she was in love with me. He kept asking questions that I didn't have answers to at the moment. I was in so much pain I really didn't care. In my mind, I knew this was the end of my career.

Megan and my mom stayed by my side the whole time. My mom met her, and my mom said that she wasn't impressed but because I liked her, she'd like her. *If this is what you want then so be it.*

The guy who was driving the transfer truck came in a little bit after my surgery and brought me flowers. He was apologizing to me and he said *I'm sorry, it's like I lost control of the truck and could not steer it.* He gave me the number to his job. They said that once I came out of surgery and was recovering to give them a call. They wanted to talk over terms with me. He said *Your doctors bill has been paid in full so no need to worry about that. My job took care of everything so whatever you need it's already taken care of and I do apologize again* he said.

He looked at my mom and he said *I do apologize for hurting your daughter. I tried everything I possibly could to stop the truck, but it did not work. For this I am very sorry.*

She looked at him and said *It's okay, you came to apologize, that's all that matters.*

Megan was like *I hope that you do not drive that truck again, the truck is very dangerous. This could have killed her, you know.*

He looked at her and said *I know and I'm sorry. It was not my intention to hurt anyone.*

I stayed in the hospital for almost two months. There was complications that had arisen that I did not anticipate nor did the doctors. They had told me that my broken ribs would heal themselves and I didn't need to be operated on, but they didn't realize that one of the ribs was floating in between my stomach and my lower abdomen. It had caused some damage, but they had gone in and fixed half of the problem.

The other problem was that one of the floating ribs was really floating and they couldn't find it. The fancy machines said that it was in the lower area but it was just moving all over the place and by the time they went in, they said that they didn't want to disturb anything so they had to leave it and couldn't do anymore. So they wanted to keep me into the hospital to monitor me and make sure that it didn't puncture anything or rupture anything that was vital.

People from the truck company came by at least twice a week to see if there was anything that I needed. This was cool at first but then I just felt like things was just getting out of hand, so I asked what is it that they would want from this situation. They offered me a settlement, to settle out of court. They said they didn't want a lot of people in on this, so they wanted to deal with me directly.

I asked my mom and she looked like she don't

know. She's like *Maybe we should get a lawyer* then they kept coming in and actually questions saying *You don't want to take this to court because it would be quite lengthy and your children would miss you.*

I told him *I needed time to think* because I really didn't know what I wanted to do at this particular moment. This was actually the first time I've had to do with anything with the courts besides going there for my traffic ticket when I was sixteen for driving on the wrong side of the street.

So as weeks went by, I told him that I would get back with them before I left here and let them know what my decision was. I still had a couple more weeks before I could be released. I took that opportunity to look up my rights and rules and regulations that went along with this court proceeding.

Being most of my family are in the law background and legal field, it wasn't hard to get people to tell me exactly what I needed to do and how I needed to go about things. They gave me some good advice. They told me that if I wanted to do this right I needed a lawyer. I didn't think I needed one but then after going over everything I decided that I do need one. But I didn't want to pay for one to figure out whether or not I really need it one, so this was a back and forth thing in my head for now.

Then I got a bright idea. I thought, well, why not just have one of my family members do it? Because they know me, they know what I need, and they're not going to charge me an arm and a leg just to try to get whatever it is that they think I need out of it. And they already have money so they don't need my money, so it wouldn't be like I'm over here trying to rob Peter to pay Paul.

So, I asked one of my family members and they was like *Okay*. They took the case, which was fine because the case was mostly already done. I did majority of the work for him so all he had to do was put his John Hancock on the paperwork that I'd already filled out.

The settlement was done, the deal was over, and I had already taken the settlement that they had offered and I even asked for a little bit more due to the fact that if you was going to settle out of court then this is the way that we was going to do it. I was going to do it by my terms and my terms only and they said *That is fine* and they did agree to everything that was in the terms. They even threw in a little extra which I didn't even have to pull their legs to get. They gave me $110,000 plus an additional $30,000 for my mom for her mental anguish and suffering, because they hurt her kid.

I had asked that they would give me installments of my money: $30,000 now for my mom and $50,000 right now for me, then $50,000 one year later, then $10,000 for the final year.

It was my passion was to be one day be a lawyer. I wanted to help someone who was in need. I wanted to be like my uncles and aunts who were in the legal field. I saw how they were, and they saw how passionate I was about law that they even offered to show me the ropes. I had a cousin who would come home from the military. He was in the military police and would bring his military law books for me to read. He saw the passion in me for law and every time he will come home, I would grab his books and read them.

Megan was there she got upset she's like *Why didn't you ask for more? You could have asked for more than that. In writing you get the whole thing at one time.*

I said *No, because I would spend it all at one time.* I

did it that way so my kids will have money when they need it—not now, but when they need it. She was upset that I gave my mom $30,000. But like I told her, that was for my kids and that's also for her going through the anguish of thinking that I was dead.

I knew what I was doing. I had it all planned and mapped out. I had time to think. I didn't go into this lightly. I didn't go into this fast or quickly, I took my time. I took a whole two months to figure out exactly the right dollar amount, the right plan, and executed it exactly the way I needed it to be.

It took me four months to get back at peak performance. After trying different methods to walk better and going to different doctors to see what I could do about the anguish of my leg I realized that one leg would be shorter than the other and there was nothing that I could do. Even though people couldn't notice, I didn't want to go outside because I knew.

CHAPTER 5
The Shunning

On the fifth month after the accident, I decided that I could no longer keep staying in the house and needed to get out and do something.

Back at my job, I was having issues with one of the men. He was trying to show me that being a lesbian was not a good thing for him. I told him that me being a lesbian has nothing to do with him. It had everything to do with me loving women. That has nothing to do with him. So I asked him *What is my sexuality doing to you?*

He stated that, by me being a lesbian, it was making him feel threatened and not a man.

So, I asked my boss, *Could I move from the*

location I was in to another location and find new orders?

My boss told me that there was none available and there was nowhere for me to go. This provided him opportunity and motive to try to get me to change my mind.

Over the next two months, it had got bad. I was harassed, fondled, spit on, and almost raped. And when I brought it to my boss's attention, he stated that if I wanted to get anywhere in life I would have to learn how to live in a man's world and stop trying to be something that I wasn't. He said that being a lesbian didn't sit well with most of them in here and that I should change who I am to fit in to their standards. And if you want to keep your job you will keep your mouth shut and stop complaining about shit that doesn't matter to you.

By the time I could spit out what I was going to say, there was another boss coming in the door who heard the whole thing. He took me aside and he said *So what has been going on?*

I told him the whole thing. I told him how I told my boss about what was going on and how he told me that I had to suck it up and keep doing my job and that there was nowhere else for him to put me because he said that nowhere was open. I told him about that almost-rape. I told him about the harassment. I told him about all the stuff that the other man was doing to me and he said *And what did your boss do?*

I told him my boss didn't do anything. I told him that *My boss told me exactly what I just told you.*

As I was telling this boss what was going on, he was on the phone with the Human Resources Department telling them about the things that was going on. He asked me who was the key players in this and I gave him each and every one of the names, even the guy who almost raped me.

I told him my boss was in the next room when it happened and when I reached out towards him he told me *Get back to work and stop fooling around.* So if anything would've went down he would have been right next door listening to it and not doing one thing about it. I knew that I was on my own and I knew I wasn't going to get any protection from him. *If you did not walk in, I wouldn't have had anyone that would know what was going on. I am grateful that you walked in when you did because who knows how much longer this would've went on.*

The Human Resources lady talked to me for about an hour. I told her everything that went on and all the stuff that was happening in and around the company. She told me *Things would be fine,* but she had to run it over with her boss to see what things would be done. Just as she was saying that, there was another woman who was coming in that was having the same issue. She said *I can vouch for what was going on with her. That is going on with me.*

The HR lady said *Now something has to be done because there's two of you.* By the time the end of the week came along, I found myself being distant and shunned by the other employees—mostly all males. The female employees tried to embrace me as much as they could but this didn't work due to the fact that the men had already shunned me and made it hard for the other women to come and be okay with what was happening.

I went home that day thinking that things would be okay and stuff would get done. I walked down to Megan's house to see what was going on and how she was. Then I got a phone. The HR lady told me that she tried my house phone but I didn't answer so she decided to call me on my cell.

I said *That is fine* and said *What is it that you need?*

She said *Please do not go to work tomorrow, she's lying. For the time being you have been suspended due to pending investigation.*

And I said *Well I need to go to work. I need to work.*

And she's like *That's fine but you cannot go to work right now.*

I asked her *Was the other men on leave as well, as I am, or am I the only one that is on leave?*

She said *No, the other men are not. They're still at work.*

I said *So how come I am the only one that has to miss work and be on leave until the pending investigation is done and over with when the men who did this to me is not on leave or pending the investigation? Is it this company's policy to make the victims feel like they have done something wrong? Well, they shouldn't have came forward in the first place, is that what message this company is trying to send? Because that is the message that I got. I shouldn't have said something then I would've been able to keep my job. This is a bad message that you're trying to send to all the female employees: If they have a* problem, they need to keep their mouth shut and not tell anyone.

With this company having well over six hundred women employees, this was bad news for them. It was actually bad news for me, too, because I never stepped foot back into that job again due to the fact that they found video evidence of the transaction that had happened in the other room while the other boss was there watching on video and they said nothing. But they told me that they would settle if I did not return. The company offer me $45,000 to leave and never come back, and to never speak of this again and or about their company.

They offered me a full retirement benefit with 10% for myself and 100% for my child. She said that there was only two offers on the table. It was that one where I took the $45,000 with full retirement with 10% and 100% for my child. Or walk away with nothing. But either way I wasn't able to go to any base in the United States, Puerto Rico, Hawaii, or Alaska, ever again.

Megan and I went out to eat dinner. I never told her what had happened, I just told her that my job was calling me to let me off and told me not to return. She thought I got fired but I never told her what had happened.

This was getting crazy to me, so I just put the money in the bank and let it sit for a while. I had learned from the first settlement that I couldn't trust her around my money or anything.

This was kind of bad for me because I didn't know if I could trust her or not. She knew nothing of the things that I did. This was making me feel like that I needed to figure out where I was headed. This was getting crazy between her and I. I was thinking that maybe I need to rethink meeting her family and friends.

Two weeks later she came home telling me that she got fired and couldn't return to work due to the relationship. This was bad. We need a break.

Later on, Aiki was sitting on his couch and Jimmy comes rushing in to him and says *I want to have a getaway, we all should go somewhere fun.*

I said *Okay, where should we go?*

Jimmy suggested *We should go to Cancun. The sun is out often, and the food is so good. Great bars and night life there.* Jimmy's like *Get your ass off the couch and plan this damn thing.*

Aiki is stoked as he jumps on the couch. Jimmy goes over there and pushes him away and Aiki said *Okay, man, I'm getting up now.*

Megan comes in and said *What you bitches doing?* Jimmy said *Aiki going to map out a trip for us and we're all going to have fun. Aiki call the boys and tell them we're going on a road trip.*

Aiki is on the computer looking for the best price to Cancun. He found a route that was the cheapest. As he was looking at prices the computer shudders and Aiki hits it and says *Darn computer.*

I said *Don't you be beating my computer over there.* He looks confused and I come up and say *Bro what's the funny look for?*

Aiki says *Well the computer found the cheapest flight and hotel but now this site looks totally different. Same time but just a different place. You heard of this site?*

I am like *Heck naw but if it's cheap who cares.* I looked at him and said *You're bugging out man. I never heard about that site but we're getting a good deal. So no worries.*

Jimmy wanted to know if that's the right spot. I was still like *It will be okay. Lets eat and sleep there and go see things around the area. It will be fun.*

You worry too much, Aiki Jimmy said. *Look for hotel and a place to eat then send it to all of our phones.*

As Aiki sat at the dinner table he was like *Something don't feel right. There's no mention of this place on the map or the internet. It just gave us the cheapest flight and hotel.*

The hotel came up after he printed the map out. This made him very intrigued. The hotel and the diner were a few blocks of each other.

Megan yelling Aiki's name. He turns to her in a dazed and cleared his throat. *Oh yeah what is it that I missed?*

She sat down and said *Where was you?*

Aiki looked at her and said *I was just thinking. This website is not on Google. I hope we don't lose our money.*

As everyone is coming to the table, Aiki and Megan is talking about where he was spaced out at in his head. Aiki is still talking about the dead website.

I sat down and there was a spider on the wall and I was freaking out. I said *Oh hell no, someone save me.* They all looked over at me and said *What the hell you talking about?*

Megan was like *Don't be such a bitch, Joe. I am*

the girl here. I was just about to get up and go to the bathroom. When I came back to the table the spider should be gone. I was waiting on one of them to get it. I said *Nothing will be done till it's gone.* Now I yelled *Get it!*

We went to Cancun and the flight was okay but the hotel was something from out of this world. The first night was crazy. We were having fun until things got real that night. When I turned around everybody was having some kind of issues. Brian got off the plane with all of us and he said that he was going to check in and meet us back at the front of the hotel so we all could go to the restaurant together.

We all met at the front of the hotel besides Brian. We waited there for about an hour for him. We asked the hotel manager if he could open the door, so we can see where our friend was. He told us that he couldn't let us in but we could leave a message.

We looked all around everywhere for Brian. We decide to call the police and get some help. Aiki and I went to the store to get some beer and drinks. We went back to the hotel to wait with Jimmy for the police in my room.

I laid across the bed while waiting on the police. I fell asleep but then I suddenly heard a squeak and jumped up, thinking it was the police. I look over and saw Aiki looking out the window sipping on his drink. And looking over at Jimmy in the kitchen trying to fix something to eat. I got up and head to the bathroom. I was in there for all of two seconds and heard a loud bang on the door. It was the police banging.

We waited for almost two hours for the police to show up. They came and said that we have to wait twenty-four hours before we can make an official report.

The police said as they were leaving *We have to take the stairs because the elevator is broken again.* As the police got close to the elevator and the stairs, they heard a loud banging. I cam a little closer to the door and heard it very loud. We heard someone say something but couldn't make out the words or the voice. It was muffled. The police called the hotel staff to see if they could call the elevator repair man. And make it fast. He told them that there was someone in the elevator and they need help. He also called the ambulance to just in case they needed medical attention.

It took two hours to get the elevator fixed. Then

all of a sudden, they got the doors open. Brian was in there, scared as all get out. He looked at us and said *What took you so long?*

I said *Man, we looked for you everywhere. What you doing in there and not partying with us?* We told the police this was our missing friend and *Thanks for your help.*

That night we went to the beach and a nice restaurant and got familiar with the area. We saw a show on the beach and then went to a bonfire that night. It was so much fun.

The second night, we woke up to the lobby being filled with water. There was a big hole in the ceiling and the water was coming down from it. We had a natural waterfall! It was so big, and the hotel manager said *Oh, we had a cave-in. No worries, it will be fixed.* This was weird because we asked the hotel manager *Could we move to another wing?* and he said the whole hotel was filled.

Then they were doing construction on some of the rooms, so we were constantly hearing banging all day and night long. That wasn't a good or pleasant thing when we're trying to sleep.

The third night we were there, the elevator

broke again. Then they decided that they wanted us to walk up twenty three flights of stairs because the elevator wasn't working, but we tried to get into the other elevator.

We did have fun, we just didn't have it at the hotel. We were there very minimal due to the fact that everything was messing up there, so we stayed gone. I would make sure whole day was filled with something to do till the we hours of the morning.

We decided that we wanted to go see a live show that evening. Megan said she had got a sunburn and that she couldn't take it anymore and she needed to go back to the hotel because she was blistering.

Then Aiki said that Jimmy bit him on the butt and made these big huge teeth mark on him. Then Brian said that he couldn't sit down for a while because something had bit him on his butt, and he didn't know where it came from. Then there was me—I felt like I had a hangover from hell.

We all stayed at this live show. I couldn't even tell you what the show was about but we was there. Everyone thought that we saw Cher, then people thought we saw Elvis, then somebody said that they thought they saw Céline Dion. I think we was all blonde or drinking too much that night because this had us going crazy. Then we laughed at the show all the night long. As we was leaving we saw at least twenty Chers walking down the street. They were dancing and having so much fun. So, we decided that we were going to follow all the Chers.

CHAPTER 6
The Nightmare

We finally found out where they was going. There was a nightclub called Nice on Ice. We got in there and at first we wasn't feeling kind of comfortable because everybody stopped and stared at us. Then we realize that there was two other rooms in the back. The first room, there's nothing but straight people there, just dancing, ordinary, looking like they weren't having fun. Then you get to the back and everybody is dancing and having fun. Now this was my type of party. I jump right on in and I decided that this was the most fun I've had since I've been here. My friends was like *What are you doing?*

I said *I'm buying the bar.*

Jimmy said *No, you're not buying the bar.*

I said *I am, and I will.*

He said *What are you doing?*

I said *This is strip club right?* So I asked the man *Can I buy the girls and the club for the night?*

He told me it was $15,000 a night.

I said *Okay, now get everyone but my boys out the club and let's do this.*

The man looked puzzled but once I showed him the money, he was like *Okay, everyone out, the clubs being shut down for the night.*

I bought it for the whole night into the day. The dancers was so tired but it was worth it that day.

When I seen what I had did the next morning, it was crazy to me. Why in the hell did I buy a bar? And shit I had a whole trunk full of alcohol. The man said I had to take it all with me. *That was crazy* my friends said. *What made you buy that bar* Aiki said?

As we were getting ready to leave, the hotel manager said *You should stay another day.*

I told him *We must get back to our side of town. We will be back, it's so beautiful here. We had so much fun and I did some crazy stuff.*

As we got back, we all went to my house to sit and talk and get us a drink. We all needed to relax and have a little more fun before we went our own ways.

Megan stayed with me and she said she wanted to make me dinner tomorrow. She stayed so we could go to the store in the morning.

We met a guy at the store while we were shopping for dinner. His name was Eric. He was a short buff guy with a short fade and light skin. He had hazel eyes and a half beard. It looked very weird, but I was like, *Okay.*

Soon as she saw him, she got googly-eyed. She was like, *He is so cute.*

I said *Yeah if you like that kind of stuff.* I know that I'm her first girlfriend, so I did know that she is bisexual and like men also. So, I knew that this could be a problem if I let it.

She walked up to him and started talking to him. She was like *We should chat sometimes.* Well I walked up and grabbed her from behind to show him that she was mine and he needed to back off. Well, that didn't work.

We let the store and went home, and she was like *Wasn't he cute?*

I said *No, not really, but you seem to think so.*

She was like *Are you jealous?*

I said *No, but why do we have to talk about him for almost an hour now?*

She was like *We weren't talking about him for an hour.*

I said *We been talking about him since we got home. You have started cooking and almost done now and we're still talking about him.*

She looked at me and said *Fine, let's change the subject then.* She went to cook and came back and asked *Should we invite him over for dinner?*

I ask her *Do you want to invite him over for dinner?* She said that it would be nice to talk with other people for dinner. I looked confused and was thinking this could be crazy. But trying to make my woman happy, I said *Dear, do what you like.*

So, the next day she invited him over for dinner. We ate and it was nice at the beginning, then he went to the bathroom. And she followed him. I sat there for a moment and then I got up and went to the back and saw them kissing and touching. I asked her

Was this what you had planned all along?

She looked at me and said *I want both of you.* This did not sit well with me. I was upset, and she was like *If you don't want me to fuck him I will not.*

I said *We didn't talk about this at all. Don't you think we needed to talk first before you just do this?*

She said *You knew I was bisexual, and you knew one day I would want to be with a man again, right? You had to know that. So I can do it now or do it behind your back with you not here. Either way I'm going to sleep with him. But wouldn't you want to be here and enjoy yourself too?* As I came closer to her she said *This will make me love you more.*

I was thinking *How will this make you love me more?* But I went alone with it and afterwards I regretted it. This became a weekly thing. I didn't like it but I wanted the woman, so I went along with this.

He told Megan that he wanted her all to herself and she should leave me. Before long he was trying to push me out. He walked by me and said *You don't have long, you will be gone soon.*

I told her what he was telling me. She was like *He knows where he stands with me, he knows I'm your woman.*

I said *No he don't know this. He keeps telling me that I don't have long.*

She said *Don't worry about him, you worry about us.* This worried me.

I came to her house one day early and she was upset with me and told me that she needed time to think. Eric was there and he was laughing. She called me later that day and asked me why I told Eric that I was thinking of cheating on her.

I was like *What in the world is going on?*

She kept yelling at me and I could barely get a word in at all. *I didn't tell him anything, I barely talk to him, so when could I tell him anything?*

He said you told him this in passing.

I said *Woman, use your head. Why would I tell that man anything about you and me?*

The next day I went over there to talk to herand she was ironing her clothes for work. We was talking and things was going well. Then I was sitting in the corner in the chair by the window and there was a knock at the door.

Eric came in and came straight back into the room. He saw me and started to yell at Megan. *What is she doing here?*

Megan looked and said *Wait, that is my girlfriend, remember?*

He said *You told me you broke up with her last night.*

Eric, I didn't tell you that. Why are you saying that?

Megan we talked last night and you said that you wanted to be with only me and not her.

I looked at her and asked *Is this true?*

She looked at me and said *No he is lying.*

I said *I told you yesterday he was lying and you said why would he lie? So I'm asking you again why would he lie?*

She looked at me with those big brown eyes and said *You don't believe me?*

I said *It has nothing to do with believing you, it's the principal that you didn't believe me yesterday. I wanted you to see how it felt.*

I was sitting in the chair and was getting up to go to the other room. He grabbed my arm and said *Where you going?*

I said *Where in the hell I want to go.*

He yelled at me and said *No you stay here.*

I asked him *Who do you think you are to me?*

'Cause you're not my man or my dad so you can't tell me where to go or come.

Eric said *No one is leaving here.*

Megan ran to me and he grabbed the iron and hit her in the arm and hit her finger that was on my arm. She looked at me and yelled *What are you doing?*

I said *What, what are you talking about?*

She asked me *Why did you do that?*

Do what?

She looked at me and said *You hurt me.*

I said *No I didn't hurt you, this dude still has me.* I asked him *Let me go.*

She's like *No you can't leave, I'm going to call the police.*

I'm like *What in the hell is happening?*

She's like *You're abusing me.*

Girl, I am not doing that. Why are you saying this?

While Eric was holding me in the room, she went to get the handcuffs. She cuffed me to the bed till the cops came.

Eric came to the bedroom when the cops got there. He uncuffed me and said *Say anything about the handcuffs and I'll kill your girlfriend.* So I kept my mouth shut and went with the police. I was release on my own recognizance.

I didn't got back to Megan's house for a few weeks. She called me but I was too mad plus the court date was coming up. So I waited till the court date to see what the out come of this would be.

Day of court, my sister and mom was in the court room. My mom said *I told you that she was bad news.* And she said *That boy looks like he is up to no good. Watch out for him, he is evil.*

Well, the judge came out and he heard few cases before mine. I waited in anticipation. I was nervous and didn't know what the outcome would be.

The judge called my name and my lawyer was in the room. He said, *Just plead guilty and you'll get less time.*

I looked at him and said *I didn't do anything at all so why would I plea out.*

He said *Because you're black and you have to have some type of time so just plea so you get less time as possible.*

I looked at him and said *No I will not. Not guilty plea for me.*

He said *Okay, this is your death sentence not mine.*

So the judge said *What is your plea?* and before my lawyer could say anything I said *Not guilty, Your Honor.*

He said *You're being charged with a felony. You understand the charges and the amount of time you're looking at, right?*

I looked at him and said *Yes, I do understand.*

The judge asked Megan to take the stand. She got up there and would not look my way until the judge asked her *Do you see the person in the court room who hurt you on that night?* She was hesitant and looked over to the bench where Eric was, then she glanced over towards me and pointed to me. He said *Can you tell me what happen on the day in question?*

Megan told the judge that I came into the house, upset about her new boyfriend, and that I didn't understand why we had to share her. She said I was sitting down, then I got up and took the iron off the ironing board and hit her on the arm and hit her pinky finger and broke it. She said that then I grabbed a knife and cut off her breast. She said *I asked her to give me $50,000 and I could get a new one* but I said no.

The judge looked confused and he said *Let's see the pictures from the hospital visit that day. Let me take a* look at the bill I have here. Okay, he said, okay, I see the arm and I see the pinky finger but no breast. Now where is the breast picture at?

She said *They did not take one.*

He said *Why wouldn't they take all of the trauma pictures for your case? Why that one was omitted?*

He asked her several more questions and then said *I reserve the right to re-examine you. Now let me hear from your witness who was there at the time of the crime. Eric can you please take the stand* he said. He asked *Do you see the person in question here today.*

Eric looked at me and smiled and said *Yes she's right over there.*

The judge asked him *Can you tell me what happened on the day in question?*

Eric said *Yes, my girl asked me to come over because her girl was coming, and she knew they was arguing that night before about me and she wanted me to come over just in case something happened. I came over right after work and Joe was sitting in the room on the chair. They were in the room talking and then I seen Joe get up and walk over to the iron and grab it and hit Megan on the arm and then hit her finger. Then she went to the kitchen and grabbed a knife and cut Megan's breast. We* told her if she just paid the $50,000 she wouldn't have to pay the doctor bill for the breast.

The judge asked *So where is the bill for the breast? And the photos if you have them. I know you took some to record the incident. Everyone takes photos to show off the battle scars. So where is the breast picture? Was the iron on?*

Eric never answered.

The judge said *Looking over the records, there is no record of the breast being even mentioned here in this case until today. Who did you tell about the cutting off of your breast? Okay, Megan, please return back to the stand please.*

As Megan walked slowly back to the bench, she turned and looked at me with a slight frown on her face.

The judge asked her *Tell me why was there no mentioned of the breast till now, the day of the trial?*

She said she told the detective about this and she doesn't know why there's no record of it in the papers.

He asked *Do you have the doctor's information that worked on your breast when this happened? Do you have his number or can you get me his records?*

Megan said *I think he moved, I don't have it.*

The judge asked her *Why would she do this to you, you think?*

With a squeaking voice, Megan said *She just wanted to taste me one more time. She needed to put my finger in her mouth.*

The judge asked her to repeat herself. *Now you say what?* She repeated herself and the judge said *What is going on here?*

My lawyer finally stood up and said *Clearly, they can't get their stories together. We're here because of the iron and not once have I heard anything but that she picked up the iron and it landed on Megan's arm somehow. Eric never answered whether the iron was on or not. There were no burn marks on any pictures, if Megan was ironing her shirt, like she said. Also, Megan said that my client bit her finger. So which was it? Did she bite the finger or did she hit the finger with the iron?*

The judge turn to Megan and said *Okay, so now the questions been asked: What was it, did she bite your finger or did she hit your finger with the iron?*

Megan looked confused and looked at Eric and started to cry. She made a loud sobbing sound and was softly saying *I'm the victim here. Why am I being* questioned? Shouldn't she be up here answering the questions?

The judge looked at Megan and said *We're asking because you and your boyfriend came up here giving different accounts to the night in question. We want to get to the bottom of the issue that is at hand. We don't want to charge Joe for something that she didn't do.*

Megan jumped up and yelled *She did do it!*

The judge said *Okay, then the burden of proof is on you. Give me something to go on.*

Megan's lawyer looked at the judge and he said *I am taking myself off the case, your honor. I can't keep this up. I am done.*

As the lawyer walked out, the judge said *What's really going on here?* Eric got up and said *I'll take the lawyers place* and the judge said *No, you sit right there.* Eric sat down and the judge said *The detective that had been on the scene, I want you to take the stand. Megan, you may have a seat with a notice to be recalled.* She looked scared as all get out but she walked fast back to her seat.

The detective came up, sat down, and looked at the judge. He said *I have given you everything from that night—it's all in the report. There was no mention of any breast being cut or hurt in my report. The only thing that was mentioned to me was Joe hit Megan's arm with the iron and then hit her finger, which did not break. It was bruised but not broken and there wasn't a burn mark where she said the iron hit her. The iron was hot when we got there—that's in the report, too. It was on setting six and hot on the ironing board when we got there. I do not know where or if the breast incident happened because that was not reported to me that day.*

The judge said *Thank you for clearing that up for me. I wanted to make sure what was going on here. Now I see clearly what's happening.*

The judge asked me *Now would you like to tell me what really happened?*

I asked my lawyer *Should I get up there and testify?* He said it couldn't hurt at this point. So I got up there and told the judge *Megan is my girlfriend and I went over to her house to talk about us and to see where we were going due to the fact that she was sleeping with Eric.* I told him *We had a argument about Eric and how he told me that he was going to get rid of me. He made up something so we could argue abut it so she would ask me to leave. He told her that I was going to cheat on her. She said go. I did and I called and asked if we could talk the next* day. She said yes and to come over after work.

I did go over and that's when I sat in the corner and she was ironing for work the next day. We was talking and that's when Eric came knocking at the door and came back to the bed room. I was still sitting and then I was getting up to leave and Eric grabbed my arm. As you can see from the photo in the case, my right arm was bruised and had a hand print on it. Those are my photos.

And then he picked up the iron and was going to hit me so Megan came and grabbed my arm and the iron hit her, but didn't burn her. Then he came back again to hit me, and he hit the finger along with my arm. Then as all that was happening Eric said that he called the cops while he was on his way there. Eric handcuffed me to the bed till the cops got there.

The judge said *You were handcuffed to the bed.*

I said *Yes, sir. I was till just before the cops came in.* Eric said that if I say anything, he was going to kill Megan. I didn't say anything.

The judge asks me *Is the truth?*

I said *Yes, this is what happened.*

He looked at Megan and Eric and asked *Was this what happened?*

They both looked at each other and said *No,*

that's not what happened.

He asked them *Where are the pictures of the breast you said was cut off? And which breast was it?* One had said left and the other said right.

He looked at me and said *I am going to dismiss this because them two cannot even agree on the breast that was cut off.* The judge looked back to Megan and Eric. *You two must stop this and don't do this again, if either one of you come back into my court room I will make sure you serve time.*

I left the court house and headed home. My boys were already there waiting. We partied all night long that I was a free woman. My mom and sister came in and said *I hope you learned from this now.* I was in love with this woman and didn't know what to do about it. My mom and sister would not understand.

Megan came back around few weeks later. We talked and she said that she still loved me and wanted to be with me. I was still in love with her, too, so we started off slow. I didn't stay at her house. I didn't go there for about three or four months. She was kind of sad about it but I said I could not trust coming over there and going through the same thing all over again and deal with your boy.

She said *You don't have to deal with him anymore.* She told me that after the court hearing, Eric started acting funny. Talking about how he was a lesbian and I had her head wrapped so tight up her ass that it wasn't funny. Two weeks later he started hitting her and making her eat another room while they ate dinner. She said that he was being really rude and mean and he also pulled her hair and dragged her down the hall and her son came home and saw this and tried to help and her son got hurt really bad. She said *I should have listen to you and left him alone but he was so fun and I wanted to be with him. I didn't see him for who he really was.* She told me that he also told her *Yeah, I told her that if she said anything I was going to kill you.*

I hate that this had happened but it made me realize that what I was feeling at first about her was right. She was someone I had to watch myself around. That was sad but it was the truth. I still didn't go over to her house. We'd just been chilling at my house.

I thought I was going to be ready to go to her house but I wasn't. My mom said that I was crazy for dealing with Megan at all, but I was in love with her. The craziness that was going through my head about her and how I felt about her was something I'd never felt before—not even with my husband so I guess this was my very first true love .

Megan wanted me to meet her family. I didn't mind. I was actually eager to see who she grew up with and where she grew up with and who were her family base here.

I was kind of nervous meeting them because of all the stuff that we had just went through and that was making me very leery of the situation.. I wanted to know what they was thinking about the situation, what did they think of me before and after the situation. I wanted to know if this was going to be a good meet and greet or was this going to be something different . I guess this was something that set my mind really heavy as the day got closer for me to meet her family that was local.

I met her brother Dan. He was pretty cool. He comes around every once every blue moon so it's not like he was in her life all the time. He would show up when he needs money or food, that was basically it. He was really strung out on drugs—this made him very unpredictable, she said, and unreliable and she didn't keep him in the house for long or by himself.

Now, I met her uncle Newton. He was nice and very sweet at first. We went over to his place a few times before he started to go left. One day we went over to his house and he asked me *Could we have a threesome together?*

I told him *No, that's not how I roll and that is your niece.*

He's like *Well, what if we take her together.*

I was like *That's not nice.*

I told Megan what Newton had said to me and she was like *Oh, he would not never say that.*

I was like *Well, he did.*

That was our very first argument that we had. It was very weird that this was happening at this particular moment because I was telling her exactly what was happening and she was telling me how sweet her uncle was and I was like *Yes, Newton is a sweet man but this is what he's telling me.* How could I get my message across without sounding so mean or harsh or unhuman and tell her?

Every time she decided that she wanted to go over to her uncle's house for dinner or to play cards I'd opt out. She didn't understand why and I was telling her *This is the reason why I feel very uncomfortable* with what is happening.

She was like *No, my uncle's not like that and he's very sweet—he wouldn't hurt a fly. You know he likes you a lot and he think the world of you. He thinks you're the sweetest woman ever. So why would you think that he would try to do something to you.*

I said *It's not that—it's how he makes me feel and the things that he has said to me. I do not like it and I'm telling you that I feel uncomfortable.*

She said *Just give him one more chance and I will definitely make sure that you're okay and if you're not feeling comfortable, we can leave.*

Believing her, I went over there and he had a party. There was a lot of people there. Newton put his hands on my leg and he was saying all kinds of lewd rude things to me, like he's was going to get me. This made me feel very uncomfortable and I went up to Megan and I said *I would like to leave.* I said *You can stay and I'll just leave on my own.*

And then she's like *No, just give it a couple more minutes. I'll be ready in a minute.* I went back to the front room to sit down. Everyone was in there dancing and Megan was in the other room with the music and the bar where her uncle had his liquor at.

She was pouring herself another drink and I was in the front room, closest to the bedroom.

The next thing I know, Newton grabbed me by my arm and pulled me into the bedroom. There was a couple of people who saw him do this. He pushed me to the bed and knocked me out. When I woke up to my pants was off and I was bleeding everywhere. Megan came rushing in and she's like *What happened, what happened?!*

I said *Your uncle grabbed me and pulled me into the room and the next thing I know I woke up like this.*

She's like *My uncle did this? He couldn't have, he was out there the whole time with us.*

I was like *No, he did.* I said *I am going to go to the hospital.*

She was like *No, if you do that I would never talk to you again. My uncle would never do that to you. Are you accusing him of raping you?*

I said *Yes, that's exactly what he did. There is no accusing, I am telling you that that's what he did to me.*

There was two guys that was standing by the door. They was like *Are you okay?*

Megan said *My uncle did not do this to her.*

The guy said *Newton grabbed her and pulled her*

into the room and pushed her down. Whatever happened after that, we don't know. He shut the door.

She's like *My uncle's never done anything like this before.*

I said *Well, this is what happened and I'm leaving.*

I got to the front door and her uncle was like *Don't you ever bring your ass back here again to my house. You're not welcome.*

I said *Don't worry about it, I will never come back here again for any reason.*

As I'm walking down the street heading towards the bus I see my friends and I tell them what happened. They wanted to go confront him and I was like *No, just take me to the hospital.*

I get to the hospital to do a rape kit. I told them who the perpetrator was and the nurse said *You will never get a conviction from him so you might as well drop it now. You have to be very careful, this is not going to go over well.*

I asked her *How do you know this?*

She's like, *I have a cousin who this happened to not too long ago and the police officer told me we were wasting our time because Newton will never get convicted.*

I asked *Why not?*

She said *Because he is a police officer. For many years he was the chief, to be exact, so they overlook everything that he does.*

This makes me sad. I say *So what justice will I have?*

She said *Honey, there's no justice when it comes to him. You just have to stay away from him at any cost.*

I said *Well, I'm dating his niece, so how do I get around that?*

She says *You just going to have to leave the niece alone because this is only going to get worse, trust me.*

I tried to break it off with Megan a few times and things just got out of hand. What went from a perfect relationship turned to a nightmare. She began to come over to my house and fight me. She tried to assault me with a poker arm. She walked all the way down the street with it to my house and my neighbors came out and try to stop her before she got to me but she struck me in my lower backside. I got thirteen stitches from that. She got mad because I wouldn't fight her back and then she said that I was being a pussy. I told her *I'd rather be a pussy then to try to keep going through this mess with you.* I stopped opening up my door for her so she took upon herself to bust through my door and break it. My dad always told me *You never hit a woman* so I don't hit a woman.

She knew this and she took full advantage of it. I was walking home from work, just off the bus, and she jumped out of the bushes and tried to stab me with a pocket knife talking about I haven't called her or came to her house in four days. I was trying to stay away from her, not go to her, but apparently she didn't get that memo.

The more I stayed away the more aggressive that she became, fighting me every chance she got. My neighbors was worried, my friends was worried. This was crazy. Her uncle was telling people that if they saw me to let him know. Being that he was the chief of police there was not much that I could do. I couldn't hide from him for long.

She kept getting even more aggressive as time went by. Two months had passed and I hadn't been to her house, I hadn't called her or talked to her. She felt like I was avoiding her and I was mistreating her and doing her wrong. She started dating this local guy and he followed her for every whim. She said *Jump* and he said *How high?* He did whatever she wanted, whenever she wanted, however she wanted.

One day, I was coming home from work. I had met my boys, hanging out with them and went to the gentlemen's club. We headed home and I told my boys, I said *Well, give me a couple of moments. Soon as I cook, we can all have dinner together and then have a few drinks, watch few movies, and play cards.* We always get a good game going on Fridays after this bar.

As I'm walking home, I felt tug on my shirt. A quick pull with a hard twist brought me down to the ground. As I was falling, I couldn't get my balance or see who was knocking me down. I got a quick bash across my head. I didn't know who or what that was.

When I woke up, I was handcuffed to a bed, nude. I knew this wasn't a good situation I was in. I knew whose house I was in but I didn't know why she handcuffed me to the bed.

Finally, I would say it was about a hour later, Megan comes into the room and looks at me and says *You can't run from me, now you're handcuffed to my bed. No need yelling 'cause I have the music on loud and every now and then I'll vacuum so my neighbors know I'm over here cleaning. But if you start yelling, I will gag you with this duct tape.* She says *We're going to have company come over later so be on your best behavior or I will have to beat you and gag you.*

I asked her why was she doing this. *Why can't we just talked about this civil like adults?*

She kept telling me and yelling *I tried to talk to you like an adult and be civil with you. You didn't want that, you wanted to avoid me, not talk to me and leave me. So I'm going to show you that you're not going to leave me or ignore me.*

Finally, I heard a knock at the door. She ran to get the duct tape to cover my mouth. I was about to yell for help, but she got to the tape before I could yell out. She went to the door—I could see through the slit of the door she left cracked that it was Newton. As he came in I could hear his raspy voice. He said *Do you have her? Where she's at?*

She said *She's in my bed.*

He said *Good.* He's like, *Give me about twenty minutes with her and then come in.*

She said *Okay.* She's like *I'll make a pot of coffee for you and a snack.*

I could see him as he was coming down the hall. He had a swift grin on his face and his eyes was beaming wide open like he had a toy from a toy chest. He came in with a gun and sat it on the table and said

There you are. You been running from me for weeks now. Finally I have you again. There's nothing that you can do. As he went to the left side of the bed to take off his clothes, he says *Stop running from me, you are mine and there's nothing that you can do about it.*

As Newton did what he did to me, Megan came in and sat in her chair and watched it, taking small sips of coffee until he was done. Then she had her turn. This went on for hours. I passed out a few times and cried a few times, but this was just the beginning of a nightmare.

Megan reached over me and unhandcuffed me and I tried to run. Megan grabbed the gun her uncle had brought in earlier and shot me in the back. At first I thought a bee had stung me. I yelled *No, I am allergic to bees!*

She said *Bitch, you were trying to leave me so I shot you.* I turned and ran towards the kitchen to get rags. She came little closer and shot me again.

I turned around and said *What the fuck, why are you shooting me?*

She said *You're mine.* The last bullet went though and that was good, but my back was killing me and I could hardly stand up. She had nursing skills so she bandaged me up and controlled he bleeding. What she didn't know was the bullet that went in my back had bounced around till it lodged in my spine.

They left me like this, tied to the bed and hurting. She gave me Tylenol which I was allergic to. She gave me Benadryl to heal but that didn't heal at all. I was in so much pain.

I was there for two days before my friends came knocking on Megan's door and they found me. I could see from the slightly cracked door to the front door from the bedroom it was my friend Jimmy. He was looking for me.

He said *Have you seen Joe? We can't find her anywhere.*

Megan told him that she hasn't seen me in weeks. Last time she seen me was at my house.

Jimmy left. He wasn't convinced Megan had not seen me, so he went to a different precinct than the one her uncle was in and asked someone could they do a check for me at Megan's house. He finally convince someone to get a warrant due to the fact that my job said I hadn't been there, no one had heard from me, and none of the stuff in my house had been touched. The cops came to her house and they found me two day after I was shot.

I was taken to the hospital and the doctors said that the bullet had lodged in my spine and that this could have been caught if I had come in sooner. The doctor said that it was in a major part of the spine. He said *So you have a 50/50 chance of being paralyzed.* This made me mad and I was crying.

The judge wouldn't even hear this in court. He said it wasn't evidence Megan shot me. The judge asked her questions and she said that I was at her house willingly and then I wanted her to handcuff me to the bed 'cause that was our game that we played.

The judge didn't really ask me any questions about being shot. He just kept asking me, *Is this true? Is that true?* and when I said *No* he said *Hmm* and went to the next thing. There was no questions about what happened and even though I had said that I was raped they said that there was no proof that it was nonconsensual sex. He said he could not do anything about that, that I was at her house, and I've had a sexual relationship with her before.

Megan's uncle got her off on first degree kidnapping and assault. She didn't do any jail time at all.

I am sitting there with a cast on my arm and bruised and I can hardly sit down. And the judge looks at me and says those words. I could hardly breathe as he said them.

So now I went to get a restraining order on both of them. 'Cause I needed protection. I was scared for the longest time. I didn't leave my house. I didn't draw my curtains and my friends only came over in the evening now. I didn't go to the gentlemen's club any more. This part of me life was a little dull and dreary. I went to the store only if I had to. I sunk into depression and it got bad.

My friend Aiki came and he said *Girl get your butt up and let's do your hair and go somewhere today.*

He made sure that I was eating and up and dressed. He got me out the house and took me places and did some things with me. He said *The only thing keeping you in the house is the mindset you let them put you in.* He told me *Stop letting them hold your mind hostage again. Come out and be free.*

Aiki said we needed to find a place for me to stay where no one would know but my immediate friends and family. I moved, Aiki and Brian helping me. They was great help, got me all packed up and everything. They took all the boxes to the U-haul truck and placed them in there nice and neatly.

I cleaned the old house from head to toe. I even cooked them a nice lunch for helping me. We cleaned everything up, closed everything up, but there was one thing that we were missing. I had turned the keys in after I had finished cleaning and closed everything up but I forgot that I left the stove on. So we was trying to decide which one of us was going to climb through the window to turn the oven off. I looked at Aiki and I said *Well I do not know who's going to go through that window* and in the end it was me who had to climb through the window.

As I was climbing through the window I got stuck. They was trying to push me through and I was like *No, pull me back!*

They said *No, we're going to push you through, you gotta go in anyway.*

I said *No no no no stop I can't go I can't go I'm stuck on something* and we wind up breaking the hinges on the window. I said *See, I told you.*

I get in and I turn the stove off but then there's a dilemma—not only did the stove knob break off as I was trying to turn the stove off, the window completely fell in on top of me with glass shattering and breaking everywhere. This was becoming a bad deal.

I rushed to open the door to let them in so they could help me. They was too busy trying to pull the glass out of me that they forgot about the stove and it kept heating up and heating up and you could hear popping and cracking and it kept spewing everywhere.

Brian looked at me and said *You get yourself in some crazy shit, don't you?*

I said *Yeah. This is by far the fucking craziest.*

Brian got an idea. *How about we unplug it and then put the knob back on it like nothing happened.*

I said *Great idea but we're gonna do with all this glass that's everywhere?*

He's like *Well let's do one thing at a time. We can only do the stove right now, that is pertinent or we gonna burn ourselves up in the house too.* So Brian pulled out the stove, Aiki jumped behind the stove and unplugged it and we kept hearing pop pop pop pop. The glass was popping everywhere—we didn't realize that the stove had already started sizzling and had got hot up top also.

Aiki was jumping back across the stove. The plug had sparked so he wanted to make sure that it wasn't catching anything on fire. He looked back down to see glass everywhere.

Brian said *Well let's try to put the window back in the frame on the wall, at least we can do that if even if there's no window.*

Trying to put that frame back in it didn't work. Aiki said maybe we need to pull it instead of pushing and I said *Isn't that the reason we're in this predicament?* They both looked at me with a funny face and I was like *Well it is.*

So we decided to leave and just leave everything just like it was. We couldn't fix everything so we let it go. They told me that I might not get my deposit back for this place and that was fine. I couldn't find my bag—I thought I had left it in the house but I realized that I didn't even bring it out of the U-haul.

As we get into the U-haul and drive to my new place, I'm optimistic and looking forward to the future. I can feel safe and don't have to worry about them knowing where I'm at. I was scared for moment but now I feel much better. I feel like I am good.

They move my stuff upstairs, then they help

me unpack and even I cook them dinner as they was unpacking.

    The circle was complete minus Jimmy. I still didn't know where he was that day. When I finally got ahold of him he said he was at Veronica's. He came the next day and helped me wash all the dishes and hang up the curtains and drapes. He even set my bed up for me. That was sweet of him.

CHAPTER 7
Nightmares Return

Now my house was all set up and I was ready to go find me a job and something to do. I could have my house parties again on the weekends. The boys like that, they said that was so much fun and they had missed it. And I was feeling a lot better, too. I also didn't have a lot to worry because I was in a whole totally different neighborhood with different people in a different jurisdiction, so I felt more comfortable. To me, this was the beginning.

Well, I did get out. I tried to go back to work. But this was hard, because every man that came towards me reminded me of Newton. He was scary but I had to try to keep my composure. He had a scruffy beard, a mustache with a hint of gray, and a beard. He also had a big belly like Santa Claus. He smelled like lemon and cheese.

Trying to keep a job was hard for me, especially with a lot of people looking just like him. Just as I was getting over the scared feeling and coming out more, things began to happen so rapidly that I couldn't see straight. Jimmy and Aiki kept coming around the house to make sure that I was okay. This was very hard on them. They don't know how to help me.

I seen it in Jimmy's eyes that he was getting more and more frustrated. This was something that was happening more and more. Jimmy would come to the house at least twice a day to make sure that I was eating, out of the bed, and dressed. He even took me to restaurants to make sure I ate. Jimmy was at my house morning, noon, and night. He was a good friend. He was there even when he didn't have to be.

We all went back to our favorite bar and we started doing that weekly again. We had card night again and it was fun. It made me feel like I was closer to the old ways and old time before all this happened.

But little did I know that soon after Christmas things would change.

Jimmy start coming to the house more and more everyday. Brian, Aiki, Jimmy and I all stayed together. We was the best of friends and very close. Everyone knew that if they found one they would find the other.

I would often get calls from Jimmy. He had just become mayor of the town in November. He often needed guidance. Jimmy was tall, white, six foot five, but built thin. He had red curly hair with a short fade and freckles. I used to tease him and say *You might get stuck under something or in something if you don't gain a lot of weight.* He said *You keep feeding me and I will gain weight.* The girl that he was dating, Veronica, was very pretty. She was tall, with light skin, and shoulder-length hair.

Right after Christmas, Veronica and I went Christmas shopping for Jimmy. She didn't get Jimmy anything for Christmas because she said that the best gifts are on sale right after Christmas. Jimmy was heartbroken that she didn't get him anything for Christmas, but that was okay. Veronica made it up to him. She had the best gift ever and he loved it.

Jimmy had just got this new job of mayor. He was so excited. This was his dream coming true, going from councilman to mayor. He was having a peaceful day until he ran into Megan. She came to his office looking for him to see if he knew where I was.

She told him that she had some stuff of mine and she wanted to return it. She hadn't heard from me in awhile and that she didn't know where she could drop it off. Jimmy say *you can drop it off here anytime you would like. I am here from nine to five, Monday through Friday. Whatever you would like to drop off you can bring here and I will take it to her.*

Just as she was about to walk out the door, she said *So you do know where she is. If you could give her a message for me please I would greatly appreciate it. I knew we got off to a bad start, but I do apologize for us not getting along. I do hope one day that we can be friends.*

Jimmy got up from behind his desk and put his hands on both side of the desk and he said *Megan, you and I will never be friends. The only reason why I knew you is because of Joe, other than that I wouldn't take to your kind.*

She said *Well since that's the way you feel, fine. Tell your friend that I have her stuff if she wants it. She* know where I live at. I haven't moved. She has a lot so tell if she wants her stuff, she can come and get it at any time. I will not bring it here. Since you do not take to my kind.

As Jimmy was leaving, he wanted to make sure that Megan wasn't following him, so he decided to go to the bakery and a few other places first before he went to my house. He finally saw Megan while he was in the bakery, so he called me and said *I'm not coming over tonight.*

I said *Okay* and he told me why he wasn't coming over for. I was like *I'm over this. Why is this coming back up now?* Just as I thought that this was over with, here it is, back again, face to face with me.

Jimmy called when he got home. He asked me *Are you okay? You want to talk?*

I told him *No, I do not want to talk about it, but I will see you tomorrow.*

This was a hard time for me. This went well on until the spring. She was trying to find out where I was living but she never did find out where I lived or moved to. Even though she tried over and over .

Late March, I started a new job This was a journey. I felt good I didn't have any issues and it was smooth sailing. As time went by I started doing good, working and hanging out with my friends, doing different things to try again to get my life back together. My friends make sure that I was good, and I was. We hung out every weekend and we did our thing.

For the last year Jimmy kept saying *You're so beautiful, I don't know why this keeps happening to you.* He says *One day, you'll be mine.* He kept telling me that. He said *I will be there for you no matter what. I'll be in your corner no matter what.*

By the time my birthday came, things was really weird between us. Aiki and Brian was like *What is happening between you and Jimmy?*

I said *Nothing is happening.*

Brian said *Something just not right between you two.*

I said *There is nothing happening between me and him. I am a lesbian and I like women.*

He's like *Yeah but does he know that?*

I was like *Uh, we been friends for many years, he should know that.*

I tried to put as much distance between me and Jimmy as possible. I stopped hanging out with him and made sure that if I was around him that someone was around, 'cause I was feeling very uncomfortable and weird after his last remark. I had told Brian and Aiki what I was feeling and they was saying the same thing. They said that it felt kind of weird and strange when he came around, the way he was looking at me. He even told Brian one day *Don't you put your hands around her anymore.*

Brian said to him *Man, what's up with you? Like something crawled up your ass or something about her.* He's like *what is it with you and her?*

Jimmy said *There's nothing up with me and her. Just don't touch her.*

Aiki said he was told by Jimmy also *I shouldn't come over to her house after a certain time because it's not respectful.* Aiki said *Man we been coming over to her house for the last five years in the middle of the night and now all of a sudden going over to her house after certain time is disrespectful?* I said to Jimmy *Don't you think if that was the case she would have said something to us by now?*

Brian said that this was the weirdest thing he's ever felt in a long time. He's like *We always so close and now we are so far apart. I don't know what's happening to us.* Roughly around a week later after we sat and talked about all this, Davenport came back into the picture after being away healing.

Davenport came and gave me a hug while Jimmy, Brian, and Aiki were sitting on the couch. Jimmy jumped up boastfully and came over and pulled Davenport away from me. Jimmy said *Don't do that.*

Davenport looked and drew back and said *What are you talking about? Do what?*

Jimmy says *Don't hug her, she doesn't like that.*

Davenport said *She got up out of her chair and came to hug me and she doesn't like that? Jimmy what are you bugging about right now?*

I looked at Jimmy and I just walked out into the other room. I couldn't with him anymore, not at this point.

So as they was in the back barbecuing I was preparing the sides and getting the desserts ready so we can all have a nice time. I was trying to keep my distance away from Jimmy. At this point we've been friends for too long for him to keep acting this way. We had laughter, fun, and games until four in the morning, which is normally our time that we get comfortable and we make a bed on the floor and we fall asleep. When this happens we normally all sleep in this order: Aiki, Brian, me, Jimmy, and then Davenport. We usually all sleep like this on the floor in my front room, watching movies until we fell asleep, but the order had to be changed that night because I was still feeling uncomfortable. Instead, I got in between Aiki and Brian. I felt safe in between both of them. This was sad to me because we have been friends for so long that I did not want our dynamics or anything to change. This was my family. Besides my sister and brother, up here that's all I had. Them and my friends.

On my birthday, Jimmy came to my house with two dozen roses, a case of Dr. Pepper, and a lime green sweater with fluffy lace on it. Jimmy knew my favorite color was lime green so he bought the sweater and it also had my monogram on it which was nice. I didn't think much of it at the time, but then looking back at it now I understand that this was a gift of entitlement.

The month of May came around. Things was still weird but almost back to normal. I had a party at my house. I invited everybody there and we all had a good time. No one was fighting.

Brian, Aiki and, Jimmy helped me clean up the house after everyone was gone. This was a blessing because they had made a mess everywhere.

Jimmy and I, we were supposed to go out to a dinner party. This was supposed to be at his company's party. But as usual, we always encounter drama before the fun began. Jimmy's girlfriend Veronica got mad and she says that we don't talk. I said *What is it that we should be talking about?*

She says *That you are hanging out with Jimmy only. And not me and Jimmy together. I feel that this is wrong.*

Well me and Jimmy was hanging out way before you and him got together and now all of a sudden in it needs to be the three of us hanging out? And you are fully aware that I am a lesbian, right, that I do not like men at all?

She said *I am aware of that but Jimmy said that you have come on to him a couple of times.*

I said *I came on to Jimmy?* I laughed. *No, never that. I love women, girl.*

Veronica said *Well when y'all go out to the gentlemen's club I want to go.*

I told her *I do not think girls are allowed in so I*

don't think you would be able to come. You might be able to sit outside but you would probably not be able to come inside.

She said *I would like to try anyway due to the fact that I would like to know what goes on inside when I'm not there. Why are you the only girl that is able to get in there anyway?*

I didn't know what to tell her.

Jimmy's sister was about to graduate. He asked me if I wanted to go to the graduation.

I said *No, not at the moment. I do not want to go.* I said *I wanna stay home and watch TV and rest up for my upcoming work week* .

He was kind of mad but he left my house and went to the graduation. He was gone for about two to three hours. I wasn't expecting him to come back to my house after the graduation but he did.

I was like *Jimmy what are you doing here? I thought you was gonna go home out the graduation.*

He looked at me and he really didn't say anything. It was more like a growl, a howl or something. He had something shiny in his back pocket. I was trying to walk around so I could see what it was but I really couldn't see. I said *Okay so do* you want something to eat since you're not gonna talk?

    I went in the kitchen to make one of his favorite sandwiches. I made him a tuna fish sandwich with cheese. I grilled them and slapped lots of butter on them just like he likes them. Then I cut the sandwich up into four squares, put a pickle in the middle, and two black olives for eyes. I took the plate to the living room and set it on the coffee table. I was just looking at Jimmy, wondering what was wrong with him.

    This wasn't like Jimmy, so I did not know what was going on. I asked him, *Did something happen at the graduation.*

    He looked at me with a blank stare on his face and those piercing blue eyes was cutting through my deep skin.

    As I was walking towards the bathroom to use it, Jimmy grabbed me from behind and without saying a word, he picked me up and flung me across the room. I hit my head on the wall and my nose was bleeding. But he wouldn't stop. I yelled out his name as he was wrestling me to the ground.

    I said *I have to use the bathroom, please let me get up and go, what is wrong with you?! I am bleeding, let me get a rag.*

He looked at me and let me go to the bathroom. He stood in the bathroom with me. I should've run then, I don't know what I was thinking but I thought maybe something had happened at the graduation and I was going to try to talk to my friend and see what was wrong with him... but that didn't happen.

We walked out of the bathroom and he grabbed me by my throat and threw me across the room again. After fighting with him for a couple hours he finally got me close to the heater and he handcuff me to it. He ripped all my clothes off and told me how beautiful I was.

He left the room, leaving me there for about fifteen to twenty minutes. I thought maybe he was gone. But he wasn't, he was just another room doing who knows what.

I asked *Can you please let me go, please. Why are you doing this?*

He said that he told me a long time ago that I would be here and that I was beautiful, that he wanted me and he said *I can't wait anymore, I am tired of waiting.*

So after he done what he did, he decided that he was going to leave me handcuffed to the heater all night 'cause he didn't want me to run.

I stared across the room, looking at my best friend, who became a stranger to me. I was so mad at Jimmy. I didn't know what to do—we had been friends for five years and not once had anything like this ever happened. So what made this happen now? I kept asking *Why?*

He kept reply with the same answer. *You. You made me do this, period.*

The next day I woke up, still handcuffed to this heater. But I guess while I was asleep he took one handcuff off of me and just left one hand handcuffed to the heater, with a note beside me saying: *Here are the handcuff keys. Breakfast is on the table. Please forgive me. Love, Jimmy.*

I took the handcuffs off and ran to the shower to take a bath. I think I stayed in the bath for almost two hours, in total disbelief, crying and trying to figure out what should I do. Who should I tell? Or should I say anything at all?

Brian and Aiki came over that same night. They said that I was acting strange and they wanted to know where Jimmy was. I told then what had happened. They both went flying off the handle and I knew something was wrong. They said *I am sorry* trying to console me.

But consoling was not what I need. I needed answers, to know why this had happened. What was it, that this day that would happen. Brian and Aiki went looking for Jimmy. They went to his dad's house, but he wasn't there. They drove across town to his mom's house, but he wasn't there. They even went to where he was staying with his sister who graduated, but he wasn't there. They went to Veronica's house and he wasn't there either. She said she hadn't seen him since last week.

This was out of the norm because Jimmy doesn't go far. Both of them came back to the house trying to convince me to go to the hospital and I said *I don't want to go*. I got two new locks on the door and did not open the door for Jimmy when he came the next day. Brian and Aiki stayed with me. I guess they was trying to make me feel safe but that really didn't make me feel safe because I already been violated by a friend and now I was uncertain about them too.

I stayed in my house and I wouldn't come out. Aiki came almost every day to visit me. I was afraid of him and he knew it. He was there and tried to reassure me every step of the way that it was okay. He made sure that I was comfortable in every way.

There was a knock at the door. I panicked and Aiki went to the door and look thought the peephole and saw it was Jimmy. He was mad and upset. I could hear him knocking so hard on the door, the front windows were rattling and shaking, and the whole wall was vibrating. Then he walked around to the back door and knocked. The banging was so loud that my next-door neighbor called me and said someone's at your door. I told her that I knew and hopefully he will go away.

He walked around to my bedroom window and was knocking on that and the neighbor told him if he didn't stop, she would call the police. He looked at her and said *Old lady if you didn't mind your business and shut up, I'm going to come over there and get you.*

She called the cops and he was still knocking on the window and then he went to the front door again.

He was there when the cops came, and they asked him what he was doing here. He said my friend lives here and I haven't heard from her in a while. I wanted to make sure she was okay. I am the mayor and I am checking on her.

The police knocked on the door and Aiki answered the door. The police were like *We need to speak to the lady of the house.* I came halfway to the door. The officer said *Are you okay?*

I said *Yes, I am.* Then once I said that, Jimmy came up to the door, moving the officer. Jimmy tried to bust past the officer and I ran.

The officer asked Aiki *What's going on?*

Aiki said *That man assaulted and raped my friend. I don't know why he is here. He can't come in.*

The officer said *He did this to her today?*

Aiki said *No it was three to four weeks ago.*

Did she make a report? the officer asked. The officer came to the room where I was to talk to me. He asked me *What's going on?* I told him what had happen to me by Jimmy. And that I had a hard time leaving my house. And that Aiki asked me to go to the hospital but I couldn't leave the house, I was too afraid.

The officer said *I'm sorry this happen to you. Would you like to make a report?* I was very hesitant at first, then I went to the front to talk to Aiki and see what he thought I should do. I didn't want Jimmy to get in trouble, but I wanted him to stay away from me for now. The officer said *We can protect you if you want us to.*

I took the officer on his offer to protect me and that was fine. I saw the officer take Jimmy and place him in the back of the car. I was scared because I seen in Jimmy's eyes, he was mad. The officer told me I would be notified of my court date. And he said he filled out the form for a restraining order. They took him downtown and booked him.

So within a few hours, Jimmy was released and was back at the door, knocking and trying to get in. This time he was kicking the door and yelling my name, asking and begging me to talk to him and come out. He said *I am sorry* and *I didn't mean to hurt you.*

The cops were called again and this time the same officer said *What is your deal, man? Didn't we just take you downtown? So why are you back here? Why are you messing with this woman again? She clearly doesn't want to talk to you at this moment so why don't you wait till she contacts you.*

The officer knocked on the door and said *I'm sorry that this happened again. He will not be getting out tonight, so you will not have to worry about this tonight. If you have any more problems, please call us again.*

I looked with tears in my eyes and scared out my mind. I didn't understanding what's happening here. Why is my friend is doing this to me? Why is he trying to talk to me when he already knew what I went through. This didn't make any sense to me. The officer tried to give me some encouraging words.

A few weeks went by and the court date was coming closer. Jimmy's dad called and asked *What's going on?* He just heard what happened. He said *Jimmy said you had him locked up for no reason.*

I told him *Jimmy raped and assaulted me so that was a reason. Ask your son what he do to me.*

He said *Jimmy didn't tell me anything about that. He just called home and said he needed bail money. I asked him why he was in there and he said you put him in there.*

I told his dad that I didn't want to talk anymore I needed to go. I was feeling very sick. I couldn't deal with this.

Brian came over to sit with me while Aiki was at work. He kept me company. But I wasn't feeling well so I went to lay in the bed all day. I was so dizzy and had nausea bad. But I was thinking this was from the stress of everything.

Later that day, Brian and Aiki took me out to eat. I was so hungry. I ate three plates of twelve chicken wings and fries.

Aiki said *What's going on? Wow you ate a lot.*

I said *Yes, I am so hungry. I don't know why.*

We went home and was playing cards. We had a good time. I forgot all about what was happening. It was like the old times and this made me happy.

The next day I had to go to the store and then go with my mom to her doctor appointment. As we were waiting on my mom to be seen, I was feeling hot and very clammy. I walked up to the counter to see how much longer. I stood there for a moment at the window and then I fell down at the front counter. I had passed out. I woke up in the back and the doctor ask me *Could there be a chance you could be pregnant.*

I told him *I don't think so. Yes maybe. I don't know.*

He said *Let's just make sure just in case. Let's be safe than sorry.*

So the nurse told me to pee in a cup and to give blood. I did. She also told me *This will take about an hour.*

My mom was in the next room getting checked

out and I was like *Let me go in with my mom and I'll get it done later.*

The nurse and doctor said that they could see both of us in the same room. *That's fine.*

I went in there with my mom. I hadn't told my mom about Jimmy because she was already going though her own stuff and didn't need to deal with my issues. I sat and told her that Jimmy had raped and assaulted me and it's possible that I may or may not be pregnant.

She asked *Why you didn't tell me?*

I explained that I didn't want to hurt her, that she already had her own issues and I didn't want to add to it.

The doctor came back in and he told my mom to take her meds and come back in a few months. Then he turned to me and said *Well, my dear, you're going to have a baby. Based on what you said about your last period, you are almost two and a half months along.*

I looked at him and started to cry and said *No. Really?*

He looked at me and said *I take it that this wasn't planned.*

I looked at him and I said *No, I was raped and*

don't know what to do now.

He told me *Well, you're in control of what you're going to do. If you keep it or not. I will give you some information that will help you.*

So I got the information about abortions, adoptions, and even nursing my child. The nurse came in and talked to me and my mom about my options and even told me about some support groups that may help me with dealing with being raped and pregnant. She also told me maybe I should look into getting some counseling.

I didn't know what to do. I was scared and afraid. I couldn't tell anyone what I was feeling. This was so much in a such a little time for me to digest. Losing my best friend and then gaining a child from my best friend. My life was changing right before my eyes.

The next week was the trial. My mom and sister came with me to the trial for support. Aiki and Brian came also to support me. As we walked in the court room, Jimmy was sitting there in the booth waiting for me to come up to my side of the booth. It was the longest walk ever in my life. I didn't think about the other people in the court room. It was like no one else was there.

As I got closer, the advocate that was assigned to my case was there. She told me that his lawyer wants you to drop this and to make this go away because this is not good for his career. His dad was in the court room and kept calling my name. He said it so loud that it echoed all thought out the room. Everyone turned around looked at him. He was yelling *You're trying to fuck up my son's career. Why are you doing this to him, you black bitch?* He was in the back sitting with Jimmy's friends and family. There was two rows of people that was there with Jimmy's dad.

I went to sit down. And my advocate said *Ignore him. This is a tactic to get you to say something and change your mind.* She said *Once you get on the stand remember I'm here for you and your family and friends are here for you.*

I told the advocate *I have something to tell you.* She sat down beside me and I whispered in her ear that I was pregnant. She looked at me and said *Oh my, this makes things more difficult now. You must tell the judge this. This will make a difference.*

I looked at her and said *I don't know if I should*

say anything. I haven't even told Jimmy yet that I was pregnant.

She reached over to touch my hand and said *Honey you don't have to tell him. He did this to you. Now is your time to get your retribution for what he did to you. And now not just you but your child also.*

I thought about what she was saying to me but it was hard to get past that this was my friend who did this to me and he was mad at me because I don't want to talk to him.

The judge came in and ask us all to rise. And as I rose up, the judge asked me to come to the front table and bring my advocate with me. Then he asked Jimmy to come up to the other table and he ask us to sit.

The judge said *So Jimmy you're being charged with rape and assault, how do you plea?*

He answered *Not guilty.*

I was looking around and I realized this wasn't like a traditional court room. There was something different about this. I kept asking my advocate *Is this how this is supposed to go?*

She told me that the court was close due to the fact that Jimmy is the mayor and the judge thought it would be best if the media and other people stay out of the courtroom.

I said *Okay, I knew something was different.*

The judge said *Lawyer, go ahead.* The lawyer that was representing me went up and made a statement and then I asked to stop him for a moment. He came back and sat down, and I told him *There was something else I need to tell you.*

He asked me *What is it?*

I said *I found out the other day I am pregnant.*

He reached in his bag and pulled out a pen and a pad to write on and said *This is good, this will help your case.*

I looked at him and asked *How is this good in any way and going to help me?* I was really getting tired of people telling me this is good. I didn't feel so good about it.

So the lawyer said to the judge *May I approach the bench?*

And the judge said *Yes you may.* Both lawyers went up to the judge. My lawyer told the judge that there'd been new evidence that was just brought to his attention.

At that moment I turned white as snow. I

shouldn't have told anyone. This would make the trial even longer. The judge says the trial would have to be set for another day because of new evidence. The judge orders a paternity test to determine that he was the father.

This was done and it came back and was sent to the courts. They asked me *Have you slept with any man in the past five years?* I told them I was a lesbian and that I only slept with one man—my husband—and that was it.

But what I didn't know was that Jimmy had written down a list of men who he said that I slept with and gave it to the courts. And because we were friends for over five years, they said that they had to contact the men on the sheet and they all had to come take a blood test. He listed my husband, Brian, Aiki, Davenport, Black, and my next-door neighbor Jackson. This was crazy to me because I only had him down on my list, but they went off of what he said instead of me.

I wasn't feeling good about this at all. I tried to just drop the charges and leave it alone because I knew this was going get crazy. *You have to go through this*, the lawyer said. He said if I back out of this now I would probably do jail time because I made a false accusation on the mayor. I didn't want that so I just stayed there with it.

This was hard for me, going through this alone. Even though my family and friends was there, I still felt alone. The lawyer seemed to be on Jimmy's side. That didn't make me feel good, either, because he was the one person that I thought had my back. He was handling my case so he supposed to be on my side. Notice I said *supposed* to be, but everything seemed to wind up in Jimmy's favor in court.

My mother and sister and friends came to court that week. They was very supportive and I was grateful for that. As I walked into the court, I knew that this was not going to be favorable for me. Everything was turning against me, and I was the one that was dying inside while everybody else was fine. My mental state at that point was all jacked up and I didn't know who or what to turn to.

Just as I was about to sit down, the judge came in and they said *All rise*. I stood there long after they said *You may be seated* thinking *Is this what I have become?* Then I finally sat down. The judge said that he had the results of the paternity of the child in question and he says he wants to take a moment to talk about the other men that was brought up doing the paternity test. He said *If you slept with all these men, why weren't they on your paper?*

I said *I only had one possible person listed on my paper and that was Jimmy. It wasn't until the next day that I found out that Jimmy had put these other men on his paper as potential fathers.*

The judge turned to Jimmy and asked him *Is this true?*

He said *Yeah, that's true. Those were the men that was around her the most, so anyone of them could be the father of her baby.*

The judge looked in disbelief like he couldn't believe what he was hearing. He said to Jimmy *You are officer of the court, you are a representative of the city. And you would put that down that the father of her baby was one of these other men besides you? Do you know how that looks? I don't know if you know, but that was tampering with evidence in an active case.*

Jimmy looked at him and said *I just told what I thought would be the truth.*

The judge said *You didn't trust that she would tell the truth in this matter?*

Jimmy says *It's not about the truth it's about what happened.*

The judge shook his head. *Just as well. I'm gonna read the results of the paternity of this child and then I'm going to read the ruling of this case afterwards.*

Now in my mind, I was thinking *We didn't even have a trial.* Everything was put on hold before we could even get the trial going, and then now all of a sudden he's gonna read the ruling of the trial and the child's paternity?

The pit of my stomach dropped and my eyes went glassy. There was a metallic taste on my tongue. I could hardly breathe and it wasn't because I didn't know—I knew it already—it was just hearing it out loud. I wasn't ready to hear.

The judge opened up the envelope. I thought it was the slowest opening of an envelope ever. It took so long for it to be pulled out, the sound of the paper made my skin crawl. I turned and looked at Jimmy and thought *Why?*

The judge finally had the paper out and he said *In the DNA paternity test in this case, you Jimmy are the father of this child.* Then he went into a spiel about how *You should take care of this child as your own* and how

The child did not ask to be here.

In the background I could hear Jimmy's family upset. His mother was yelling *I don't want no nigger baby* and *How could you do this to us* and *The baby won't be accepted into our family. Jimmy, you have disgraced our family. How can you give our family to someone not of our race?*

His dad was upset, mostly yelling at me saying *I thought you was better than this, how could you just go and get pregnant like that, you can't keep it, you can't possibly keep it, you would ruin our family, this is not who we are.* Now, this is coming from a black man. He wasn't as dark as I was, he was light-skinned. He could pass as white but you could tell that he was black. Which made Jimmy some black too even though he had brown hair, blue eyes, and freckles.

It was ruining the dynamic of their family by me having this child. I remained quiet through all the huffing and puffing that was going on in the background while the guards and the judge was trying to get everybody quiet. This went on for awhile and then the judge says that if anybody keeps talking he's gonna hold everyone in contempt of court.

The last thing I heard before the judge ordered

his mom to be taken to the back was her yelling *I'm gonna kill you and your baby*. The judge ordered her to be taken into custody in the back. She was so mad that she kept ranting and yelling *You are a dead bitch, you are a dead bitch!* This kept going on until she finally went through the door and they closed it.

The judge said *Clearly this has gotten way out of control. We can't do this here. Order in the court!* The judge said *I'm gonna make a ruling on this case right now.* I'm ordering twelve months with eleven months suspended. He said *The order for the child is that all hospital bills are taken care of by Jimmy's insurance and anything else that this child needs will be taken care of by Jimmy. Once the child is born, there will be a total of a high cap of $1500 sent per month and no lower than $500 a month.*

I turned to my lawyer. *Is this the outcome of me staying and going through this, he gets to walk away?* the lawyer says that the judge was being favorable because he is the mayor and it wouldn't look good for our city's great mayor to be locked up under charges of rape and assault. *I did the best that I could do under the circumstance. I'm sorry, honey, but this is the way this goes. Don't forget, you in a man's world, so if you need* something you just have to ask the man to help you.

I look back at my mom and my sister in disbelief while his family is still making signals of cutting my throat. Not only was I afraid, I had to ask my lawyer to stand and ask if I could get a restraining order against him and his family, and if any dealings that I needed for this child would have to go through the courts, please.

The judge said *Everything that has to deal with the child should come through the court system. All medical bills, all insurance issues, and all financial issues of the child should come directly to the courts.*

The judge ordered that I walk out first, along with my family members and friends. Since he had already issued a protection order for me, he thought that this would be the best thing for me. As I was walking out, there was a girl that was coming from the left side of me. She was coming very slowly at first but then I saw the distraction that was being made by two guys on my right. The security guards was trying to break up the fight that was happening with the two guys. They was not paying attention to me like they were supposed to.

She came from the back side of me and before I

knew it she tried to stab me in my stomach. I turned around too fast for her so instead she stabbed me in my arm. This was alarming because I knew that this was only just the beginning.

I was taken to the hospital and checked out, and they made sure that the baby was okay and that it was okay for me to leave and go home.

My lawyer called the next day and he told me that the young woman who stabbed me was hired by the family to get rid of me before I could leave the courthouse. *She won't say who hired her but we all know who did.*

My mom and sister was very fearful of what would happen and feared for my life. My mom said *You have to move from where you're living at, I know you just moved there not too long ago but you have to break your lease and leave, 'cause this is not working. You have to move somewhere where he doesn't know where you are so you can be protected and safe.*

Where I'm from black and white do not mix together and they sure as hell don't have a baby together. That was a no-no. Majority of the black and white couples from where I'm from, they normally get hung and I didn't want to be getting hung so I decided that I needed to move.

I asked Brian and Aiki to help me move. They did. This was very hard because I had just moved here, got comfortable and settled in and then this happened.

For the next few weeks my phone kept blowing up, people kept calling and calling and calling, the newspaper and the news reporters and the TV woman kept calling asking me for my story about what happened, and would I like to make a statement. I decided to change my number.

Fearful for my life, I moved into a neighborhood that Jimmy would least expect me to move into. It was okay for awhile. I had a big back porch and a room for the baby set up. I didn't know whether I was gonna keep it or give it away. My mother didn't believe in abortion so that wasn't even an option.

My mother came and saw me every weekend. My friends was down every weekend and in the week too. They kept a close eye on me but I kept a close eye on myself. It was me and Johnnie Walker, we had the best times. I was depressed. I was upset. I was mad.

Jimmy's dad kept calling and threatening me.

Finally Jimmy found me on the street one day. I guess he's been riding around looking for me for weeks. He had a bigass bag of money. He said *I proposition you, get rid of the thing and we'll never speak of it again.* He said *Here is $4000, take it do and whatever you want to do with it but take at least $1000 and get rid of that thing before my family has a fit.*

He says *You do not know how much that thing is causing a rift between me and my family. I'm not gonna do anything, I just wanna give you the money so you can get rid of it.* He's like *That's the only option. Do the right thing and don't have it. I can't be a father to a black baby.* It just better be done. *Don't make me come look for you 'cause if I have to come look for you there's nothing in the world's gonna stop me from killing you and it.* He said *I'm telling you one more time, get rid of it before I get rid of it for you.*

I walked away in disbelief because this is a man that I've been friends with for over five years and he's never had a issue with my race or color. This was very difficult to hear from him. At this point I can't believe my ears. I had no way of understanding what was taking place and what was happening at that moment. I knew that Jimmy and I would never be friends again. And the stress of this was too much for me but there was one thing that I was grateful for: that he didn't know where I lived out or didn't know where abouts to look for me. He knew that I frequently came downtown where we were at that moment and he knew that I would definitely come to this restaurant where we were at. I didn't know if I was being followed or anything like that so this was a very scary time for me and with me being pregnant at the same time.

    I got a letter in the mail from the courthouse stating that if I was having this baby that Jimmy requested to be there present at the time of the delivery. I knew that this was a way of him trying to figure out if I was having the baby or not so I figured that I just was just gonna go ahead and have this baby because there was nothing else that I could do.

    In my mind I was scared as fuck but then I realized that I had to be strong because I had a life that I had to be strong for. There was no way that I could get past this. I had to grow up really fast, my mom had my other two kids and I had to really grow up or I wouldn't make it to see the next couple of years.

    I got a job close to where I was living at so I

didn't have to travel so far back and forth downtown. That had been a lot of stress, on top of trying not to run into Jimmy or his people who were downtown. My job was by the water, at a bakery that made all sorts of foreign bread and different types of goodies and sweets.

One day I was walking from my job to the bakery. I could see in the distance there was a man with a big build, with his back turned towards me slightly. It was familiar, but I didn't pay any attention to it. I went into the store anyway.

So I went in got my sweets and came out I was heading home but before I could head home the man said *Joe*. I turned around and I looked and there was Megan's uncle Newton. He had his uniform on from work and he said *Don't run, if you run I'm gonna shoot*. So I stood there and I turned all the way around and he saw my belly and he said *Oh you have a bun in the oven I see*. He said *That couldn't possibly be mine is it?*

No, it's not yours.

He said *Oh, somebody else got that good stuff, huh. I knew it wouldn't be long, it's too good to pass up*. He said *I just wanna talk to you for moment, I wanted to see you. I've been looking all over for you. Why don't you come to my house and let's talk again?

I looked him in the eyes and said *I will never come to your house again. I don't want anything to do with you.*

He said with a smartass grin on his face *You know you want this again. It was the best you ever had.*

I told him *No, not really. The best I ever had, was from a woman and you didn't even come close to that. So I'm sorry, I won't be partaking of anything at your home.*

He looked at me and said *Bitch, do you know who you talking to? Every woman wants this.*

And I told him, *Yeah, every woman might want you. But do they know what they're getting when they get it?* I said *I have to go, I have to cook dinner, I have to catch my bus. So you have a nice day.*

As I turned around I saw the store owner looking out through the window. He barely spoke English so I knew that he wouldn't understand and come to my rescue if I called out for help. But I was gonna take my chances of walking away now while I could before he grabbed me and threw me in his truck.

As I was walking away he reached around for his gun and he said *Don't move or I'll shoot you right in* your head and then I'm gonna shoot you in the stomach.

I didn't move and stood very still. I didn't wanna give him a reason to shoot me but I wanted to go home. He said that he was gonna call his niece up so she could come and *We can all have fun together.*

I told him *I would rather run through hell then to deal with you or your niece again.*

As I was walking away, he ran behind me and grabbed my arm really tight and yanked me around. I said *If you wanna shoot me, shoot me. If you wanna talk, then talk.* I said *Either way action is going to be done.*

He looked at me and said *Get on your effing knees* and he grabbed in my head, pushing me down to the ground, to my knees. He comes around and forcefully puts his gun all around my face, pushing it so I can feel the cold embrace of the gun against my skin. Then he grabbed my hair and he pulled it, yanking chunks out of my head. I felt my head bleeding then finally he hit me at the top of my head and blood started pouring. He said *You will listen to what I have to say to you.* He said *You will always be mine no matter where you go. And whoever or whatever this bastard is, it's gotta go 'cause I didn't put it there.*

I'm on my knees on the cold hard concrete,

rocks imbedded into my knees, blood dripping from the top of my head And all I could think about was Johnnie Walker. I didn't wanna leave it. I needed to get home so I could get it. I wanted this to be over really fast quick and in a hurry one way or another.

I was tired.

He looked down at me and he said *You can't possibly think that you're gonna walk away from this. Either you gonna be mine or I'm just gonna kill you right here where you stand. So what is going to be?* He put the gun two inches away from my face and said *Are you ready to go?*

I looked at him and I said *Yeah. I have nothing to live for, there's nothing here for me anymore. So if you wanna do it, why don't you just go ahead and get it over and done with and don't be a pussy.* I sat up a little bit off the ground and pushed myself up and I grabbed the barrel of the gun and he said *Wait, what are you doing? Stop!* so I put the gun tip edge in my mouth and I said *If you gonna pull it, pull it. Don't be a pussy about it. Pull it, let me help you help me.*

His eyes got big and he was like *Stop this, stop this before you make this gun go off. Stop pulling it!* I said *You said you wanted to shoot me, you wanted to be the last person that I ever see? Then go ahead and pull that trigger. What are you waiting for? Why you keep playing around? Why don't you just help me get it over with?!*

As we were sitting there debating and fussing and arguing back and forth about me holding the gun and him pulling the trigger and him being the last person that I see, the owner of the store came out and another customer came out and they said *What is going on here?* and then Newton says *I am the chief of police, mind your business, go back into the store.*

The store owner said *This is not right, she was just in here getting bread. So what is she under arrest for?*

Newton said *She's not under arrest.*

Well, why do you have a pregnant woman on her knees with a gun in her mouth if she's not under arrest? I'm not understanding.

And then I started to laugh. I was so scared, I started to laugh. I was on my knees with a gun in my mouth, blood spilling from my face, and rocks imbedded in my knees, laughing.

Newton thought I was crazy. He said *You had fucking lost your rocker, girl.* He said *I can't fuck with somebody who is just as fucked up as I am.* He's like *You too crazy for me. I don't do crazy bitch.*

And I just continued to laugh. It wasn't funny, it was just that I could not have even expressed what was happening to me at the moment. It just came out as laughter. I was so angry, so mad, so scared, so in the moment that it just came out as laughter and no one understood it.

It was then I had reached my breaking point. I could not see that I had reached it but I had. I was about to have a baby in a couple of months and I knew that this could not keep continuing to go on. I knew that I had to at least find a piece of mind for these next two months.

I decided to move back home with my mom for awhile and be closer to my kids for the last two months of my pregnancy. I didn't know that the next two months would shape my life in a way that I couldn't understand.

You would have thought that the incidents before this had made me wake up and understand. But there was no filter for my life and there was no stopping the roller coaster that I was on.

It just kept going and going.

So, I moved back home. I lived on a very rural street where cars come down every now and then. I was walking home one day and there was about five or six people walking on the same street. I didn't think anything of it. On the corner, there was a church and then two houses next to it and on the other side of the street there was two houses and an empty lot. The intersection on the other side of the church didn't have anything there but trees, brush, and some type of metal object that was sticking out of the ground like a dome.

It was a warm day so everybody would have been outside. Just as I looked around to see if anybody was outside the people that had seen were gone, walking down the hill past the church.

I was drinking my soda, minding my own business. I hear a car coming behind me but I didn't think anything of it. It was a van behind me, with two guys and a girl. They had grabbed me before I could even turn around. We drove for an hour.

The woman that was in the van was uncomfortable with me being there and you could tell because she was fidgeting back and forth. She kept asking *Are you sure this what we want to do?*

The guy said *Yes this is what we're going to do. This is what we been waiting for, for the longest time and now she's here and this is what we're going to do.*

So she tied me to the dresser. Then she brought me some water. She even brought me some food. I tried to get free but the dresser is heavy as heck. I tried to move it but it won't budge. I can't pull it, pick it up, turn it, flip it, or do any kind of stuff to it to knock it over to get a loose. With one hand semi free, it was kind of hard for me to get away or even try to get up or down or move. Plus I was pregnant at the same time so that just made it even difficult and put more strain of pressure on me and the baby.

This was crazy because she kept coming in and out and really was worried. She kept her eye on me. Every night she came and gave me water and food while the men slept. She was really nice to me. she even sat on the floor by where I was and we talked. She said *You're not as bad as they said you was.*

This made me scared a little because I didn't know if she was trying to butter me up to get my baby and kill me. I didn't know her plan for me yet. But I did know that she was sweet to me. She made sure I was comfortable and well fed. She even made a make shift potty for me. She held my hand during all the things the men did to me.

She made sure I was okay. I was here for about a month because I had a few more weeks before I delivered.

One day the two guys came in the room, unchained me, picked me up, and took me into the other room. One guy said *We're going to blindfold you for just two* seconds. They did but it was longer than two seconds.

One guy started forcing himself on me while she was looking and then she came and moved him away. As she took the blindfold off, I saw she had two knives and a gun at her side. I realized that my hands were untied and I could move freely but if I made a move, the men were going to take me out. So I stayed very still hoping they would not notice that my hands was free. I didn't no if she untied me or not but I didn't want to get her in any trouble.

One of the guys said *Don't say a word. And don't move, this will go faster.* He looked over at her and said *Everything will be okay.* She did what she had to do and then the man said *It's your turn now.* She took her turn. She took her time. The men left to go do whatever they had to do. She was doing what she wanted to do.

By the time the men came back, it was not over

with yet. I figured one of them was her husband because he kept watching her and he got really upset and his face started getting mad. He kept pacing back and forth from the front door to the back to the front to the back and by the time she had finished doing what she was doing, he picked up the gun and he started yelling at her.

I didn't understand what they were yelling about, and she just kept saying *You wouldn't understand.* He said *You've never done that before so why now* and she said *I just was wanting to do it and this was the perfect opportunity.* He's like *Well I don't like it* and she said *I don't give a damn what you don't like. I did it.* Then he started yelling and then he grabbed her, and she turned around and she smacked him. At the same time that she smacked him, I heard the gun go off.

Now I am laying on this hardwood table with no clothes on, no shoes, no nothing and I did not know what to do at that moment when the gun went off, but I did know that was my opportunity to go.

Looking down I saw all the blood that was everywhere, and she was sprawled out and the two men was over there over top of her trying to figure out what to do. One guy went to get towels, the other guy was yelling her name and I'm sitting there frantic and scared out of my mind. I didn't know where I was at or how I was going to get away.

Then I got up and put pressure on her head while the other guy tried to get towels. Then I went and start boiling water and they was like *What are you doing?* I said *I'm helping, now shut up.* I said *She's going to bleed out if y'all don't get her to the hospital.*

The husband said *Wow why are you helping me?* I say *Because I don't want to see anybody get hurt. Let's get her up and in the van and let's go before she die.*

The guy was like *But you don't have any clothes on.*

I said *Grab my clothes and let's go.* I got in the van and they drove to the hospital. I told him *I won't say a word, I'll just sit here if you want and wait till you come back.* I said *If you want to chain me up you can but I'll be here. I don't have any clothes to go anywhere. I hate to see anybody see me nude so there is nowhere I'm going.*

I was thinking once they left, I would run and that would be my opportunity to go. I told them that they can even take my clothes with them but instead they gave me my clothes and I told me to go home. I didn't know who these people were, I never seen them before, but they knew who I was. They called me by my name and it was scary.

As I was walking home down the road, trying to put on my clothes and run at the same time, I kept hearing someone yell out *Peaches*! Now my name is not Peach, so I wouldn't think to turn around at that moment. I kept going. So as I'm still walking down the street when they yell *Peaches! Stop! Freeze!*

Now, my name is not Peaches, so I'm still walking. I realized that there was a police car behind me and a guy yelling, walking really fast towards me. He ran up on me and pulled me down to the ground.

He said *Peaches why are you running from me? You heard me call you way back there and now you have me run and put you down to the ground.*

I rolled over and told the officer *My name is not Peaches, my name is Joe and I have just escaped from being captured and raped by three people.* I said *They're at the hospital right now—two men and a woman. The woman got shot in the mouth and they're at the hospital right now.*

The police officer said What are you talking about? *Is this one of your jokes again*?

I said *No*. I said *Do you know who I am?*

He said *Aren't you Peaches?*

I said *No, my name is Joe. For the last time, I just escaped being captured and raped. Why are you not listening to me? I don't understand what's happening here. Are you not going to go and look or see what I was talking about? I don't understand why you're not going or even calling it in.*

As he was trying to wrestle me down to the ground he got up and got his walkie talkie and he said he needed backup. I was thinking *Backup for what? What did I do?* I said *I was just walking down the street and you need backup for me walking down the street?* and he said *Shut up.*

I didn't understand what was happening at the moment. He rolled me over and he said *Peaches is you pregnant? When did you get pregnant, we just took you into custody last week and you weren't pregnant. What happened, how did you hide it from us?*

I said *I am not Peaches, for the last time.*

He looked at me and he said *You're Peaches. That is your name. What you trying to do is get out of being arrested.*

They tried to wrestle me down to the ground again but I was already there with my head down on the ground. My belly would not let me lay flat on the ground. They don't care at all. They started beating me with these sticks. I don't like it so I grab one. I was like *Stop, you going to send me into labor* and then one of the guys said *I thought you said this was Peaches.*

The guy said *This is peaches. She just got thick and extra fat within a couple of days.* Then the backup for the backup cops he said *She's not going down, she's strong as an ox, what's wrong with her. I don't know* the first one said *Maybe she's been eating a lot? I told you she got really big over the couple of days that she was out.*

And they was still trying to restrain me down to the ground. They thought I was resisting arrest when I kept telling them that my belly was hurting and I need to get off it and I was moving from side to side and they just kept thinking that I was resisting arrest.

When the fourth cop car came, he said *What is the issue?* He's like *We have four cop cars for one girl? What is happening, why can't you just put her in the back of the car?*

The one guy said *We tried but she's strong as an ox and she's actually got extra stuffing, she ate really good since she's been out.* By then there was eight guys holding me down. They said *It got very much out of* hand. The chief finally got involved and he said *Stop. Pick her up, don't worry about putting handcuffs on her, just pick her up. Stand her up and let me talk to her.* He said *What is the issue here?*

I said *I was walking down the street minding my own business and your officer was calling out Peaches. And he thought it was me but my name is Joe. I told the officer that I had been held captive and raped and the three people who did it are now at the hospital down the street from here. The woman got shot by one of the men and they're at the hospital. They let me go when they went into the hospital. Then the cops knocked me down to the ground and tried to put handcuffs on me when I was trying to tell them what was happening to me and then they kept saying that I was this other person when I wasn't.*

The chief said *Okay, do you have an identification?*

I said *I don't have anything. Do you not see what I have on? I have a shirt, socks, and man shoes on. I do not have any identification on me because I am trying to run home after being kidnapped.*

The officer said that he couldn't let me go, he had to take me down to the station and book me under not having any identification on me. Until they figured out who I really was they was not going to let me go.

I got downtown. I was fingerprinted and booked on a charge that belonged to someone else and with no identification. The only thing that saved me was my fingerprints was not in the system and they couldn't understand why my fingerprints wasn't in the system. I had to wait till the next day to see the judge and I explained to him and told him this exact same story that I told the chief of police. The judge asked the police officer *Did you check out her story?*

The police officer said *No because we thought she was Peaches and we didn't think to look.*

The judge said *Well you have thirty minutes to figure out whether her story is real or not.* The court adjourned back in thirty minutes and the police came in with their findings. The judge asked *What did you find?*

The police officer said *We found what she said was the truth. There was a woman that was into the hospital for a gunshot through the mouth and two men accompanied her. We sent three officers down to the hospital where the woman is in critical condition.*

So, you mean to tell me the judge said *that you*

have woman who's been raped, who told you that she was RAPED and captured and instead of checking it out, you booked her and put her in a cage and left her there all night?

The judge turned to me and apologized and told me I was free to go. I went in the back and got processed out and was let go.

After leaving the jail I went home to try to sit and process all this that was happening. I knew I had to make a move, I just didn't know what I needed to do. Not soon after I had just sat down I heard a knock at the door. I look through the peephole and I saw that it was Jimmy.

I yelled through the door *What do you want?* and *How did you find me?*

He said *I found that out through the registry of the jail.*

I said *Why are you checking up on me? Why are you stalking me? I had asked for a restraining order, why you not obeying it?*

He said I do not have to obey it. I just need to know where you are, and did you do what I asked you to do? I gave you money to do what you needed to do. Is it done yet?

I said *No.*

He said Are you forcing my hand? Just be expecting me, any time and any place. You will not know when I will come or who I will send to take care of y'all. I'll be back. Don't worry, I'll get you. And don't forget to renew your driver's license next month with your current address.

I got scared and started freaking out. I didn't know what to do. This was getting out of control. My life was heading into a whirlwind. I knew I had to do something, I just didn't know what I needed to do. The next day I was heading to work, and I heard someone yell my name. I turned around and it was Jimmy. He had a gun pointed out the window of his car. He shot in the air one warning shot then he charged towards me with the car, almost running me off the road, almost hitting me if I didn't jump onto the curve in between two cars. This was terrifying to me to know that he was trying to kill me and my baby. We have been friends for so long and this is the thanks I get.

This had continued for almost a week and a half just right up until I had my baby.

I went into labor and by the court order I had to call and let him know when I went into labor. So I gave him a call to tell him that I was in labor, and his dad said that he was busy out playing golf and didn't want anything to do with any black baby. I called my mom and my sister and had them come up to the hospital as fast as they could, so if anything happened, they would be there.

After I had the baby, there was a woman that came in. She bought the baby Pampers, clothes, food, everything that it needed. She said *If you ever need anything call this number and the baby will have whatever it needs.* She even said that *By the end of the week the baby will have a steady income. She is already been taken care of.*

There was a lot of complications with the baby and I tried to keep optimistic approach. My mom wanted me to see if I could get some help. My baby didn't cry, my baby really didn't do anything but just sat there. When the baby was born, I really didn't want to touch it, but I did.

That night, a woman came into the room. She walked right up to me and pointed the gun straight to my head and said *This is for Jimmy.* Then she looked over to the left where the baby was laying and then she looked at me and then she looked back at the baby. She's like *What's wrong with it?*

I said *I don't know yet, I'm trying to wait for the doctors to tell me exactly what's wrong.*

She looked at me and she said *I'm sorry.*

I said *It's okay.*

She's like *I was never here, just like I'm going to tell Jimmy that I could not find your room and they sent me to the wrong room. I don't want to be responsible for killing a special baby. I can't have that on my conscience. You won't have to worry about me. You will not see me ever again. Sorry to bother you. She's beautiful, by the way. She looks just like Jimmy.*

Yes, she does.

She left, and I took a deep breath in really hard and a really fast exhale out. I knew that I needed to do something before someone else came back. Since she didn't finish the job. This made me very fearful of what could happen if he sent someone else back.

I pressed the button and ask the nurse, *Could I be released tonight? It is an emergency.* I made up a story, so I could get out and leave early. I left and I ran to my mom's. I went down there and stayed for two days.

Before I knew it, Jimmy was standing outside

of my mom's door. I was in the basement. I was down there and I tried to keep the baby as quiet as possible while my mom handled the situation.

He said *If you find your daughter please tell her to call me, I am looking for her. I have something for the baby.*

She told him *Okay, if I hear from her I will let you know. You know how she is, she would take off in a moment and leave and I won't hear from her for years. So when I do hear from her, I will let her know that you came by and you were looking for her and have something for the baby.*

I knew at that moment I had to find something or somewhere to go to be safe.

I left my mother's house. I told her I would let her know where I was at when I got settled.

I stayed in any place no more than a month. I didn't know who I could trust or whether someone was after me. This got a little tiring with a baby, trying to keep her away from an invisible enemy was hard. I called my mom and let her know where I was at often and she would tell me that he came by or called. For months he would call at least four times a month As time went by he would call two times a month. Then he got to the point that he would come down there to my mom's house and sit across the street and just watch. I really didn't know what to do about the situation but to run.

Then my mom got a call one day from Megan saying that Newton was looking for me. He thought that he had seen me and she wanted to let me know that I needed to be off the streets if I was up there and to get somewhere safe because he was looking for me and he was on a rampage that he thought he saw me. So not only was I running from one man but I was running from two.

I moved to Florida and then my mom called and told me that Jimmy said that he knew where I was at and he was headed my way. I asked her *How did he find me?*

She said that she didn't know. I knew I had to leave left everything in my apartment and took only what I could take for the baby and a few things for myself. I went to another state and this time I knew that I had to keep it light and be under the radar. At that point I knew that he was looking really hard.

After that I went to many other states. I couldn't figure out how he was finding me. I was really scared and alone running with the baby and trying to make sure that my other two kids that were back at home were safe to with my mom. I was not only worried for them but I was worried for myself.

I was walking out of my apartment one day when I saw Jimmy standing across the street. I don't know how he found me, but he looked at me and said *You can start running now. I found you and I'll make sure you and your baby's bodies get back to your mother.* He shot four shots and I knew it was nothing but God that was protecting us. As he aimed the gun toward us, he could not have been more than twelve feet away cross the street. He shot directly at us and no bullets touched us—they went around us.

When I turned around the bullets was lodged in the wall on both sides of me. It was like it was pushed into the side into the wall behind me. I had to go—I didn't know where to go—but I knew I had to go.

This man was really out to get us. He really didn't want a black baby. This made it very hard for me to comprehend how we was friends for so long and I did not know that he was secretly racist. I was trying to protect my child from her own father who wanted her dead—something that you would see on TV, not something you would imagine going through.

I was on the edge of breaking. I couldn't see my way out. But I knew that I needed to protect this little one more than I needed to protect me.

CHAPTER 8
The Magic

I knew this was the beginning of the end. I couldn't tell you how many nights I stayed up watching the door wondering when or how my life would end. I knew that moment after leaving my friend that I would have to make life changes if I was going to live to see twenty-five.

I kept running from state to state to state because nothing felt safe. The more I ran, the more I needed to run. My mind had been completely overrun by two men. I let them defeat my mind. I had no time to think for myself because I was always in that fight or flight mode. This made it hard for me to see where I was headed because I was blinded by fear.

This time I made a big move. The move was to a state that I felt at home at peace and safe. I met this girl who show me that I could be anything I wanted to be—anything but afraid. She taught me that by being afraid I would have let them win. She said *You can't do that—you have to fight.* She took me to her house and let me stay there for a couple of weeks until I could get on my feet and I did. She said *No one has to know you or know anything about you I want you to get yourself together. Because you have a child you can't stay here in this terrified place. There's no need for you to wallow when you can stand on your own two feet.*

That month I found a place this stay and a job. I even enrolled into school, trying to get my mind off of the things that was happening to me. By then, my child was two. I still called my mother twice a month to check in. I called her from a throw-away phone because I didn't know if my phone calls were being tracked.

I tried to do everything I could to be very careful, to make sure that we were safe. I eventually brought all my kids to me. This was the beginning of our life together. I moved to a neighborhood that was kid friendly, so my kids can have other kids to play with. They made friends in the neighborhood and so did I.

I enrolled in a local college. I was going to school and working part time. I got comfortable here in the state. I worried but not as much as the day before.

As time went by, I still called my mother to make sure things was okay. I was in school and learning how to trust my instincts and my surroundings. In the back of my mind, everything I did I always had to think twice about and look around to make sure that I was safe. Even though I had to live like this for a while, I figured that I could live my life. I decided to try to take my life back and not live in so much fear.

This was the best thing that I could have ever done because I started living for the very first time. I became free and started seeing me in a whole different light. I wasn't running away from me anymore. I was embracing who I was becoming. throughout this journey that I was going through.

I was meeting some incredible people. They would help me throughout this journey that I was going through. I would get up every morning and take the kids to school and then go to my school where I met Fred, Alex, and Steven. These three was like no other. They had my back long before I even knew who they were.

An incident happened at my school. There was this woman and this guy—they came out of nowhere. One guy was in the corner, trying to talk to me, and I told him *Listen I don't even do men like that so back off.*

He kept telling me *You don't know what you had. I could change your mind.*

I said *If that was the case, my husband would have did that a long time ago. No, thank you.* And he just kept on not realizing that there was a woman that was sitting across the room on the other side watching the whole thing. So then she comes up to me and she tells me *You're beautiful, let's hang out sometime.*

I said *No, not interested, thank you though.*

She was like *Oh, you trying to be a stuck up bitch.*

I said *No, I'm just not interested in hanging out with you.* Little did I know that she was friends with the guy that was harassing me. I got up and went out of the room. I decided that I had enough and I was going to go home but that's not where it left off.

They followed me, as well. The guy was

yelling, saying *You dyke bitch* and calling me all kinds of names. And the woman was yelling *You stuck up.*

I said *I'm not stuck up in and I'm not a bitch, I just don't want to be in the companies of you. And if I am all these things, why you trying so hard to get me to change my mind? You're out here now, yelling at me, calling me names, doing all this when you could've just left it all alone and go about your business. If I'm all of those things, why are you here?!*

That's when I saw Fred, Steven and Alex. They was coming up the tunnel and saw what was happening. Instantly Fred stepped in. He said *What is going on here?*

I said *These two people are trying to get to see their side. One is trying to get me to go out with her and another one telling me that he could change my mind from being a lesbian.*

Alex laughed and said *Dude, you know, if a lesbian is going to be a lesbian, she's going to be lesbian always.*

What in the hell are you talking about? the guy asked. *Lesbians, they like men too.*

Steven said *That is just the stupidest thing ever. Bisexuals like women and men, not lesbians. Don't you* know anything about women?

The guy says *Yes, I like women, so I know everything about a woman.*

Fred said *You can like women all you want, that doesn't mean you know anything about women. And clearly you don't know anything about women because lesbians only like women, bisexuals like women and men, and she's clearly not bisexual—she looks like a dude. She's one of us, so why are you jacking on her if she don't want it?*

I turned to both of them and I said *Thank you but no thank you, I'm out* and I started walking away. I told Fred, Alex, and Steven *Thank you for your help* and *I hope you have a nice day* and I started walking away.

Fred started running up behind me. He said *Wait, I don't know your name.*

I said *My name is Joe.*

He said *Joe, we're going out for couple drinks tonight. Would you like to join us?*

I said *Sure. Where would you like to meet at?*

He said *At a local bar around the corner. We could go there right now. I could take my stuff to my car and we can be on.*

I was in favor of that. I had nothing else to do

until the kids got home from school. I didn't want to start drinking today again, so I told them *Well, let's do something else besides drinking* and we did—we went bowling after the bar. They said this was the best thing that they could do because they was going to drink, they said.

It was getting close to the time to go home and pick the kids up. I said *I will see you again later at school.*

They said *Yeah, let's hang out more. This seems like a fun thing to do and you are cool people, you are so much fun. We have to do this next week during the weekend, so we can let loose and let our hair down.*

At that moment I did not know that Steven was gay. I didn't find that out till later, but it really didn't matter to me because he was cool people, whether he was gay or not. I started going out more and doing things with my new friends Fred, Alex, and Steven. They were great guys. We had a lot of fun and went a lot of places. They gave me a peace of mind that I could trust a man, at least a little bit. I wasn't all the way there but at least I found the group of men that I could trust halfway.

I didn't tell them about the ordeal that I was running from. I don't want to get them worried, all caught up in my drama, so I just told them *We have to be on the lookout for my ex-husband.* I didn't want to tell them everything what I was running from. I just wanted to be friends with them and be okay without the drama.

As months went along, I found a job at a local store. I would go to this coffee shop that was right around the corner from my job. Always went in there because of the sweet-smelling aroma of cinnamon and vanilla. This made me come in there even more but there was one thing that keep me coming back even more.

There was a beautiful girl that came into the coffee shop every morning. We met there every day before work. She ordered the same thing: a vanilla latte with no whip cream and a vanilla bean on top of the cup. I tried to get there early so I can get a glimpse of her walking in, so I can let her go first. She was tall with a slender body and a bronze glow. She has brown eyes with wavy shoulder-length black hair.

I got behind her as she walked up to the counter and got a whiff of her perfume—the sweet smell of flowers and berries. She had my senses going wild. As she got her coffee and was walking out the door, I said *Have a great day.*

She turned around and said *Oh hey, thank you. Same to you.*

This was the first time I said anything to her. This was a good start. Maybe tomorrow I could say a little more.

I got to work and thought about her all day long. I wish I knew what her name was. I wish I knew where she worked so I could send flowers without her knowing it was me.

I got to the coffee shop early the next day, so I could see which direction she was walking from, but I didn't see her today. She didn't come at all. I waited for an hour for her to show up.

I went to work and called a few of my friends to meet me at the club. I needed to clear my mind. This was much needed since for the past six months I have seen the most beautiful woman ever and suddenly poof! She's gone.

At home, I was playing my music and getting dressed and getting ready to go. I'm looking so good. I have on my denim blue jeans and a black shirt with a yellow logo on the front. I have my yellow and black shoes on and yellow socks. Yes, I am looking so good.

Maybe I will meet someone and hit it off.

My phone starts ringing of the hook. *It's Joe.* Steven was outside and ready to go. As I grabbed my coat and keys, I see the coffee shop logo and think of the beautiful woman that I see there.

As I get in the car, Steven says *What are you doing man, you are looking good. Are you trying to fry some fish tonight?*

I looked at him and said *Fry fish? What in the world are you talking about?*

He said *You want to meet a girl, man, that's all.*

Oh yeah, I am trying to catch one then.

We get in the club and we meet up with Fred and Alex. They were already there waiting. We danced and drank for hours. Then, across the room, there she was sitting there with three girls. She was laughing and then she pointed to me. The girls looked and was smiling. She got up and walked towards me.

She said You're the cute guy from the coffee shop, right?

I said *Yes* with a squeaky voice.

She said *So why have you not spoken to me before yesterday? I see you always wait till I go and get my coffee and get right behind me, when you clearly were there first.*

That's so sweet and nice of you to do that. I did notice all those things.

So, what's your name? I ask.

She told me *My name is Jasmine.*

I said *Nice to meet you, Jasmine, nice to meet you. My name is Joe.* I took her over to the bar and brought her a drink. We danced the night away till my friend Fred got into a fight with someone at the club.

Steven came running up to me and said *Help.*

I said *Please excuse me, let me see what's going on.* Got there and saw Fred was on the ground and a big dude was over him. I pulled the dude off him and got in between them. Got Fred up and took him to the other side. The dude came up and said *I'm gonna get you.*

Then his friend said *Chris, he's not worth it, let it go.*

Jasmine's friends came to her and got her. She didn't want to leave me. She told her friends *Wait, let me see if he is okay.*

Her friend Amber said *No, don't get involved with that.*

Jasmine's like *No, let me go see if he is okay.*

As I get Fred straight, Jasmine comes up

behind me and grabs me and asked if I am okay. I turned to her and pulled her close and said with a strong voice *Yes, I am.*

Everyone got into the car and headed back to my place. I couldn't believe she convinced her friends to come back to my place. Her girlfriends with my boys. We get there, and everyone brought something to drink, and I order something to eat.

Everyone is having fun. The party is going to the pool. One of the girls took off her top and bottoms and jump in the pool nude. I said *Well, guys, that's how you start a party.* They all jumped in but Jasmine and I.

We went to the couch and talked for a while. We let everyone else do their own thing. She was amazed that I never said anything before yesterday to her. She said *I was waiting on you to say hello or ask me my name, something.*

I was like *I was afraid to say anything. A pretty girl overlooks guys like me.*

She said *I noticed you the first day but as months went by I just let you do what you was doing. I seen you was there first, and you let me go and got right behind me. To me, that was sweet* she said.

We were drinking and talking and we forgot

about the others. She said *What does your room looks like?*

I said *It looks like a white room with four walls and a TV and a bed.*

She's like *Okay, smart ass. Take me to your room.*

We laid on the bed and talked some more. She ran her hands up my thighs. I got nervous and jumped up and asked her *Do you want any more drinks?*

She said *No, silly.* She grabbed my hand and pulled me on top of her, running her hand along my back. She pulled off my shirt and unbuckled my pants.

As we laid on the bed, we fell asleep in each other's arms.

I woke up later with a hangover. I felt something in my bed beside me under the covers. I see long flowing hair. I am sitting here thinking *Where did she come from?* So, I slowly pulled back the covers and saw it was Jasmine. She was still here in my bed. I was amazed that she was still here. Then I got a flash back from the club and I smiled.

She woke up and looked up at me smiling at her. She said *How did you sleep?*

I slept great and you?

She said *I slept wonderfully. This was the first time I slept in a man's bed and didn't sleep with him.*

I said *Is that a good thing?*

She was like *Yes, very much, it was a good thing.*

I was getting excited just by the glimpse of her. I pulled the covers closer to me. She got up and went to the bathroom and I tried to get myself to calm down. Then she came out and she said *Do you have eggs?*

Yes, I have eggs. You want me to go make you some?

She said *No, I'm making breakfast. You go take a shower.*

She went downstairs to cook and I got up to take a shower. I couldn't get up until she left the room. I was too excited.

I got out the shower nude as hell and about to get dressed. I was running to grab my towel to cover up.

She came in and she said *Sit down and let me feed you.* I sat at the table in my bedroom with my towel and she served me a plate and gave me a strong cup of coffee. She cooked bacon, eggs, grits and pancakes. Wow, it smelled so good. Almost like my mom cooking for me on Christmas Day.

I waited for her to fix her plate and eat with me. It felt good to eat with her. We talked and laughed about everything and nothing at the same time. This was different to me. I'd never had a woman cook for me before, so I didn't know how to act.

A soft kiss on the cheek and she went to take a shower. She came out and asked how my food was. I said *It was delicious*. A woman that could cook was amazing to me.

We got dressed and was thinking of things to do today. We went walking on the beach and just had a good time, laughing about everything and nothing at the same time. This was the best day I'd had in a long time. It was all smiles from ear to ear for me.

As time went on everybody was waking up and getting dressed after the night before. I'm glad everyone had a good time. I did for sure.

After that night seeing how beautiful she was, I was wondering *Was this going to be just the one-night hook up?*

Jasmine came over and sat beside me and said *Where would you like to go for lunch today?*

I said *Anywhere you want to go, miss lady.*

After everyone had left, my friend said that they would call me back later to see how I was doing. I grabbed my coat and put on hers.

She was like *Let's go to a place that you haven't been before.*

I said *Okay, that sounds like fun.*

She's like *As long as it's not too crazy, I'm down for it.*

We went to this place, it was a very fancy restaurant too. It had a waterfall in the middle of the room with a roaring fire that came out of a dragon's mouth. There was flowers all over the place, well decorated. I felt like I was in a movie. She had picked this restaurant and it served her well too.

She had good taste, the price was great and everything looked very appealing. The waitress had on a nice fancy dress and her name tag was in gold. I was very much impressed with the surrounding and ambience of this place.

Jasmine ordered something simple and basic. She got a steak with lobster tail and shrimp, with mashed potatoes smothered in gravy and asparagus. I ordered a steak and shrimp with steamed broccoli and chicken wings.

We sat and talked for a long time at the restaurant while we ate. I asked her, *Do you have a girlfriend or boyfriend?*

She said *No, I have neither.*

I asked *Are you a lesbian or are you bisexual?*

She said *I am a lesbian all the way.*

I asked *Why are you single?*

She said *I couldn't find the right one. I broke up with my girlfriend a month ago. It wasn't working out.*

I said I'm sorry to hear that but I'm glad in a way because you're here with me.

She said *Yes, you're so right. I'm looking for a good woman that I can take care of and love and be good too and she be good to me. Someone that don't play games and will be there for me as I be there for them.* She looked at me and she put her hands on my hand and she said *You wouldn't happen to know where I could find her do you?*

I turned around and said *I don't know, they're hard to find these days. When you do find them, I think you better get your fishing rod and reel, man.*

She looked at me and laugh softly. She's like *Well, I guess we're going to have to stop by the hardware* store now after lunch.

I laughed and said *Yeah, I guess we're going to have to stop by the hardware store.*

She said *I'll have to give you my number before we leave. I enjoyed sitting here talking to you for the longest time, it made me feel really good to be able to sit and talk with someone like this. I had forgotten what talking to another adult on a personal level felt like. My last relationship, we didn't talk. She came over and she left—that was our relationship.*

Jasmine said *I have a meeting at 2:30 today, but I would like to carry on this conversation a little bit more, later on. Could we have dinner together tonight somewhere? My treat.*

I said *Yes, that would be just fine.*

She said *Um, say around five o'clock or five-thirty?*

I said *Sure.*

She said *Text me your number right now. That way I'll have it and I will text you where to meet me at five-ish.*

We left the restaurant. We had a great lunch. Everything was perfect. She went her way and I went mine.

I got to work and trying to concentrate was

hard. Sitting in this meeting with Mr. Claiborne was like pulling teeth and nails because I wasn't focusing on what he was saying at all. My eyes were focused on my watch the whole time. Mr. Claiborne was still talking about *The policies* and *The rules* and *The new market picture* that we was going to plan to do later on this week. But my mind was elsewhere, trying to focus on this and think of her as well was hard.

He asks me *What you think of the deal so far?*

I said *I think we should go for it.*

He said *Well do we have a deal?*

I was like *Yes* but little did I know I was saying yes to a year contract and investment.

As four o'clock was approaching my eyes was locked on the door the meeting was almost over and I couldn't wait. Mr. Claiborne said *We will have to go over the details of this investment.*

I said *Yes, but I have a meeting at five o'clock that I have to get to. I cannot do it today. After work tomorrow? I'll be here bright and early and we can go over there investment and see where we should go.*

Five o'clock rolled around and I got a text message. She said *Let's meet at Cafe Josie's at 5:30.*

I couldn't wait. I got us a table and when she

came in, the waitress brought her over to the table. She reached over and touched my hand and whispered in my ear and said *I'll be right back in a minute.*

My heart fluttered and I had goosebumps all over. She was heading to the back towards the bathroom. She came back about ten minutes later and she was all dolled up and she had a little small box that she placed in the middle of the table. We talked the whole night away. We had a great dinner and great conversation.

She says *Now that I have something to do with my free time I'm loving it.*

I looked at her and I said *What do you have to do on your free time? I hope it's something fun.*

She looked at me and smiled and said *Yes it's very fun, thank you.* She reached over and rubbed my face and said *You are my something to do on my free time.*

I said *Me?*

She yelled *Yes, you! Hope you have a good time with me. I'm not that bad of a girl. You have those sweet looking eyes that I can't turn down, so I am here at the moment.*

As we were sitting there, my mind went into a

blank haze. I was thinking, and this was weird for me because I never really think about the moment that I'm having with someone. I just enjoy it.

Jasmine looked at me and she said *What are you thinking about?*

I said *I'm thinking about you.*

She said Me?

I said *Yeah, you. I really think you are an awesome person and this really doesn't happen to me often. I never get speechless or have nothing to talk about.*

She's like *That's a good thing, I hope.*

I say *Yes, it is a good thing.*

The whole time that I was with her I had forgot all about my problems that I was going through and have been through. My mind was finally at peace. She had made all my cares go away. This was very scary for me due to the fact that I had already been with Megan and that was a total disaster. Trying to convince myself that this was going to be different was hard.

We had been dating for about a year before I asked Jasmine to marry me. I had asked her mom and dad for her hand in marriage. We took a trip to see her dad and we stayed down there. I met him for the first time. Even though we had talked often on the phone, that was the first time meeting him. And then with her mom, we went for a drive and I asked her that way.

Her mom and dad said *Yes, that would be great.* This had made me feel so good that they had accepted me in their family.

I had Jasmine's mom set up a family gathering. I wanted everyone there at the backyard of her mom's and her dad even came in for the special day. Everything was so perfect. I got up on a platform and did a backflip off the deck to where she was standing. Her sister set it up that she would stand there and have Jasmine ready.

Jasmine said *Yes, of course* and I was happy she did.

We started our new life together and with my new investment at work it worked out great. She was so pleased to be my girl. We got married in Spring and we told the kids we were going on a road trip. We gave them a bucket of chicken and a bag of candy.

Now the trip was good, till the chicken ran out. that's when the issues came into play. They cared more about the chicken then they did the candy... so we had to stop and get more chicken.

It took us three days to get there to get married. When we got there, we realized that we was number fifty-seven of people waiting to get married of the same sex. This was a glorious day for me.

We had the wedding at the courthouse, and the children were present to be our witnesses. They were saying *Okay*, as long as they had their chicken.

This took my mind off of the things that had happened before. I had called my sister to see if anything was happening down there. She told me that no one came for a long time, about three months now.

I knew that I needed to tell my newly wife Jasmine about the other things that had transpired before. As I was telling her all the things that happened, she said she was with me through thick and thin. She gave me that reassurance that everything was going to be okay.

A few months later, my sister said that Jimmy was back down there asking questions and that this time, he was asking questions to my other family members.

I haven't been afraid in a long time, but I knew that it was about to get real again. And I was right—

this was just the beginning. This was just the start of his tries, but at that moment, I was hoping that this would be a dead end for him.

This had made me nervous again. But I wasn't going to let that change me. My goal was to stay focused and my wife helped me do that. This was the first time I didn't feel alone going though this.

I knew then that I had to make a change for the better. I couldn't let this hinder my growth. I had finally found the peace I was looking for. I didn't have to run from me or anything else matter of fact. I was embracing everything about the new me to come.

Jasmine and I had our issues, but I knew I was growing in a way that was not alien with each other. I went back to school to do political science. I wanted to help people. I felt I was just sitting here wasting away. I felt that I wasn't doing anything with my life. I knew I needed a change and one really fast. My mindset was being compromised again and this made it hard for me. The nightmares, the daydreams, and the panicking was going to be my demise.

I knew I couldn't go back to where I was before, but I couldn't stay here either. I knew I needed to make the change within myself. I started reading self-help books and reading my Bible. I had to look inside and change the way I was, before I had a nervous breakdown.

Jasmine really didn't understand that. She thought that maybe if I just went and got some help from my therapist, that would be better. I was trying to look within myself to fix me, but I did take her advice. I did go and saw somebody. I got to one of the main issues in my life. It helped a little bit but the majority of the help was when I helped myself. No one can understand what it meant to go through something so traumatic and still love people. I still think the world of others.

Even though we stayed together for a few more years, I knew the direction that I was going, she couldn't follow. There was a couple of issues that tore us apart. There will be love between us for a lifetime. We had a great relationship.

But I knew it was time to go.

After leaving Jasmine, my world has changed dramatically. I started seeing me for who I really was and becoming the woman that I am today. I knew the direction that I wanted to go, and it was just a matter of time before the pieces of me fell into place like a puzzle.

I finally got both of my degrees and graduated. I found the job that I love or close to it. Things came into perspective.

I wanted to try to run for higher office. I was two signatures away from getting on the ballot. I didn't give up, I tried again the next year. When that election was held, I still didn't get it but I wasn't about to give up. I would keep trying.

Life got better. The kids started growing up and I got less worried about the two men that was coming after me. Newton had passed away just a while back. Jimmy never stopped looking for me—matter of fact, he still looking. Periodically, my family would tell me that he had been down there asking *Have you seen her?* But nobody's telling him anything.

You would think after all these years he would give up. The little black baby is now grown up, a big beautiful black woman, who now has her own family and is doing her own thing.

And I am fine after all these years. I've learned that sometimes you just got to let things go in order to grow. I became the best me while losing me. And when I found myself, I knew that this would be a great outcome. Because with all the struggles that I had went through, I knew that one day I would be able to help someone else who was in the same situation like me.

And I did, and we became the best of friends. I knew I wasn't the only one that had went through stuff like this and I knew that I went through all these things just to help someone overcome similar issues like mine.

You see, when you change *how* you see things in your life. You begin to realize that how you live your life is a perception of what you see and feel. Then you can manifest it in your everyday life. When there's no enemy within to hold you back, then there is no enemies outside to stop you from your growth. When you let go and change your mind on how you see things, your life will change too.

I'm here to tell you, the darkness can't last forever and there is light at the end of the tunnel. I couldn't see it while I was in it but I seen it once I was about to hit daybreak. And I realize that no matter how bad the situation looks at the moment, there can always be a change in every situation. It's just how you look at it and see it. Keeping a positive attitude, no matter what is happening around you is hard. I did it in order to overcome the barriers that I had to face and the mountains that I had to climb.

Now when I look at people, I see the love in their eyes. And I see a story in everyone. This makes me more passionate and humbled to help someone else. All that time that I was going through all those issues and challenges, I saw it as a blessing. I was given another chance at life time after time after time. I am here still to talk and walk about it. I didn't have any help during those times and it could've made me bitter angry and even mad. But I chose to hold on to the love that I had for the world and the people in it, instead of making myself a mad angry black woman because the system failed me. I figured that I could be the help someone else needed.

Now I'm out here trying to help people and fix the system that failed me and failed many other people like me. I was a young child and I knew exactly how it felt to be a victim over and over again without a thought of what I really needed. I had adults tell me what they thought I needed. They would never once I ask me what I really need it.

Now I make sure that every child out there has

a voice. Advocating for children and families is what I've been doing for the last past years. I'm here to tell you that there is light at the end of the rainbow. You just got to keep holding on sometimes what is appears to be is not what it is. I urge you to take a deeper look and see what's going on around you and see what is really going on in your backyard. You could possibly help someone who is in need and is going through the same things you have gone through.

Just know that the journey that you're on is one that is yours and yours alone. The battle can be won. You just got to keep a positive attitude and your head up. Sometimes staying humble is the best way you can be. When you find that you have no one to turn too and you think that no one is listening or seeing you, know that there is someone out there that will help you through your toughest times when you are least expecting it. My past experiences were a struggle and it did teach me that no matter what issues you have going on, you can't just give up 'cause it's hard or seems impossible. It takes hard work and dedication to keep moving after something bad happens and not just give up. That's why I had to stay focused and often come out of my comfort zone. I had to push myself farther than I thought I could go.

It's not always going to be comfortable when you want to have a better life. Sometimes it will feel strange, but if this is to change your life? Why not. This is a necessary journey to a better you.

Am I where I'm supposed to be? Are events from my past making it hard to go forward? Am I afraid to go forward in life because of my past? What will my future look like if I let go of my past and make a better life for my future? These are the questions we must ask ourselves to begin the journey. To go and make a change to a start new life.

I do believe that God will send the right people and support and the right combination to you. You can overcome your barriers with the help He sends. The hurt and pain will not last forever if you let it go and move in a direction that helps you grow. Sometimes holding on to what hurt you does more damage than to let it go. I do believe that everything happens for a reason.

Everything that was in the past had to be left to begin anew. Everything that took place from that moment of chaos in my childhood to now, has shaped me to be the woman that I am today. This was the beginning and that's where this story begins... but not where it ends.

I walk in peace and love, not to hate and resentment. Because I let things go and don't hold on to the negativity and let it guide my life. I am no longer a prisoner.

Everyone is important and deserves to know that someone care for them. I did this by advocating for people just like me. Advocating for youth that is scared and alone, that don't have a voice or are scared and alone, going though stuff. They deserve to know that someone is there for them and really cares. That's why I do everything I can to help a child, because I know how it feels to want help and no one comes to help you. I make sure I ask the youth what is it that they need. I ask *How I can help you?* I let them know that I am someone who is here that truly cares.

Everything in my past led me to this moment right here. I do believe that this is where I supposed to be. Though all the darkness and pain came a light that shines brighter than ever now. I can't do anything but thank God and the few people who stood by me when it got crazy.

If you think that you can't make it, please take

a look at how far you have come and what you have overcome, to see that even if you have much more to go, it will get better as you do. This is just the beginning, and nothing can stop you from living out your dreams. Better days are ahead. Don't give up. You can do this! Believe in yourself and others will believe in you as well.

Some people love it when life is easy and perfect. You will never build yourself up when it's perfect. You build yourself when it's imperfect. This will grow you. This is when you learn who you are, when life throws you curve balls.

Being there for everyone else but not being there for you is only hurting you. If you're not the greatest you, then you're cheating yourself out of the life you could really have. Wake and appreciate every day as a gift and live. Focus on the positive that's happening in your life. Protect your peace and start your day off right. Don't let what happened to you keep you from being the true you. I want you to take your life to the next level. I want to support you on your journey and know that there's hope.

Now, I don't want you to feel sorry for me after reading this. That is not what it was written for, because I am great now. I wrote this to get my message across that you're not alone and there's someone out here just like you that made it.

I know if I had someone like me when this first started, things could have been better. Most people don't talk about multi-rape victims. There're no groups for us. There are more of us out here than you know. Know that we do exist and were out here and one day I am going to start a group for people just like us.

Sometimes fear stops us from telling our story. But you never know who needs to hear it or how it will impact someone else's life.

Thank you for taking the time to read this.

Printed in the USA
CPSIA information can be obtained
at www.ICGtesting.com
LVHW011325050824
787388LV00002B/201

9 781590 929377